Three Months in Nepal

Hazel Roy

ISBN: 978-0-9559451-0-6
Published by: Hazel Roy
in conjunction with Writersworld Ltd

Printed and bound by Print On Demand,
Peterborough

www.writersworld.co.uk

WRITERSWORLD
9 Manor Close, Enstone, Oxfordshire, OX7 4LU, England

Design and typesetting: Dominic Mandrell
proof reading and editing Jane Allen / Sue Croft

To my father, Fred Roy, 1907-1999,
who gave me a passion for theatre, travel
and social justice, and to the children of Nepal
in the hope they will build a better future.

Introduction

There comes a point in most people's life when they survey the future and wonder 'is that all there is?' Suddenly we are conscious of time speeding up and doors closing – awareness that many of our dreams remain unfulfilled and that time is no longer on our side.

It could be the death of parents, loss of a loved one, redundancy or retirement, the first grey hair, the significant birthday, children growing up and leaving home, the menopause, a serious illness – whatever the trigger, the feeling is a common one.

This book has been written about my own struggle to make use of this window of time to fulfil some of my dreams while I still possessed the wit and health to do so.

This is not just a book about travel, though I have always had a passion for new places and for new experiences. It is a diary about beginnings rather than endings. It is an incomplete story. It is about the business of taking risks, regaining self-confidence and discovering hidden strengths and talents long suppressed.

Women, particularly of my generation, have had difficulty fulfilling their potential. Part of the post-war boom generation, we grew to adulthood in the 60s. The lucky ones from working-class homes were the first generation to go to University – though in my case as a mature student with two young children.

When I left University in the mid 70s a degree was still, just about, a passport for a better paid job, but in my case, divorce determined that this had to be one with 'sensible hours,' which I could combine with all the demands of single parenthood. Living in an industrial city in the Midlands, trying to find my feet as a part-time FE lecturer, struggling to keep my mortgage paid, keep an ultimately impossible relationship afloat and combine all this with a heavy involvement in left wing politics, my early desire to work in the theatre as a professional actor soon vanished firmly out of sight.

Moves, new jobs, more beginnings and more endings left me in my late 50s, my parents dead, my mortgage paid up, my four children more or less grown up, another divorce on the way and my self-confidence at an all-time low. Something had to change.

I had for many years wanted to visit India and Nepal. Some places have a special appeal for reasons you cannot always analyse. But I had wanted to live or work there rather than visit as a tourist. I had been deeply envious of someone, at the time very close to me, whose job gave him the opportunity for remote travel to interesting places and the longing for our relationship to work was combined in my mind with a longing for the life he led.

Some relationships end abruptly. Others drag on doing terrible damage to the self-esteem. Realising I had to kick-start myself out of this low point in my life, I responded to an ad in a Youth Hostel magazine and signed up for a challenge trek in Nepal, nine months hence. Volunteering for this would require me to get seriously fit and to raise £2,000 in advance sponsorship. With a new focus in my life I began to evolve a plan to stay on and teach in Nepal till my visa expired.

I got involved in the local Nepalese Association and through them gained introductions to a number of schools in Nepal. After many e-mails I received an agreement from a very prestigious school in Patan, where, in exchange for accommodation and food, I could work as a volunteer, teaching English and Drama. It was also agreed I would participate in a morning programme for working children. I would start work there immediately the trek was over.

Looking back on the diary I kept of the trek, I am aware of how isolated I appear from the others who took part. It is not easy to form friendships with people who are much fitter than you and who, consequently you see for only a brief period each day before they forge ahead and disappear out of sight. My continuing depression did not make it easy to strike up friendships, especially when there appeared to be little or no common points of reference between us. It was only when the trek was over and I began living in the local community that Nepal began to work its magic on me.

When I went to Nepal in 2002, the country was at a turning point in its history. Since 1996, after two centuries fighting other people's wars, the Nepali people had become embroiled in a civil war of their own. With its feudal ruling structure, rampant inequality and social injustices, flagrant corruption and an expanding population sharing limited resources, the country had been ripe for insurrection for some time. The Maoists[1] called it 'The People's War' which was appropriate since it was mainly the people, often the poorest and with the least to lose who lost their lives. By 2002 thousands of lives had already been claimed.

In the outside world, coverage of Nepal's abject poverty, the royal massacre of 2001 and the news reports of the violence, had tarnished the country's reputation for tranquillity and harmony with a corollary effect on tourism. This was the background to my first visit. It was not till 2006 that the war and the power of an unpopular monarchy ended and a fragile democracy returned. If readers are surprised that war does not intrude more into my story it is because, as an outsider never directly involved, I saw that glaring inequalities in wealth were as much a cause of the war as a product, and that grinding poverty would not disappear with the end of the war, whatever the outcome.

When I started out, I little imagined what a profound effect the country would have on me. I travelled there with no special expectations about helping people or making a difference. I was simply a 55 year-old woman at a particularly vulnerable point in her life, ripe for taking risks and feeling a little reckless.

1. The Communist Party of Nepal (CPN-M) were reputed to be inspired by Peru's Shining Path rebels with the stated aims of destroying government institutions and replacing them with a revolutionary peasant regime. They represented many in the lower castes of Nepali society.

I am glad I went in a reckless state of mind because it made me more open to risk taking and challenges. I got both of those in abundance. For the first time in my life I was given the opportunity to do what I had always wanted to do. I found out what I was good at and I was able to make young people question the world they were inheriting. The legacy of that time continues, both in terms of the UK charity I helped establish on my return and in the documentation of a unique theatre project with street children - the first of its kind in the world.

Few visitors from the developed world have the chance to get so close and to uncover so much about the issues of child labour, for example. It was at one and the same time a privilege, a nightmare and a responsibility. This book is an attempt to record those children's stories so they will not be forgotten. I was given the rare opportunity to use talents I always knew I had, in a way that could make a difference and to collaborate with an immensely talented theatre director. Such chances, for most of us, come rarely in life - they should not be squandered or forgotten.

I began this book as a journal, on the advice of my tutor at Manchester University, intending to document my teaching experience as part of a research project for an MA in Applied Theatre. I also kept a chronicle of my travels in the hope that Lonely Planet would honour the literary contract they had offered me a few weeks before my departure. But mostly I kept it to document my thoughts and feelings in a very personal way. Living alone for the first time in my life in a culture full of challenges and surprises, I realised with a shock, that I was happier and more fulfilled than I had ever been, and that true happiness is not dependent on who we love, or what we own, but is within each of us if we will only care to take the risk and say a giant 'yes' to life.

Three Months in Nepal - Contents

The Helambu Trek

Friday February 15th 2002

'In February Hazel Roy will be rising to the challenge of a gruelling six day 75-mile trek in the foothills of the Himalayas, Nepal, to raise £2000 for the Youth Hostel Association 'Give us a Break' initiative that enables disadvantaged and disabled youngsters to enjoy youth hostel holidays.'
Manchester Evening News, November 2001

I stared blankly at the picture accompanying the article, self-consciously posed with a rucksack over my shoulder, in my back garden. I did not feel like a charity trekker, a supporter of worthy causes. A sense of adventure, a thirst for travel and a desire to do something useful are among my motives for going on this trek, but there is more to it than that. I am at a watershed in my life – I am going to Nepal for more than a physical challenge. I am in search of a new future.

It seems as if I have been planning this trip forever. For weeks my bedroom has been strewn with bits of trekking paraphernalia. A medical kit, a mosquito net, a head torch, lightweight fleeces, trekking poles, sun hat, fleece hat, waterproof gloves and trekking clothes all have to compete for space with more formal clothes for teaching, various TEFL manuals and books on drama games. Two full-length wrap round skirts made by a friend's daughter, a pashmina shawl, a silk sleeping-bag liner and a pair of Coolmax trousers which wash and dry in half an hour, are to prove my most useful possessions over the next few months.

My husband, absent from my life for some weeks, has obligingly offered both myself and a fellow trekker a lift to Heathrow. We are in the throes of a separation and I sense that he views my departure with something akin to relief. In the circumstances I am grateful for his offer and so is Mike from Chorley, a young post-graduate chemist with a George Formby accent, who looks suspiciously athletic.

My mounting concern had been that I will not be fit enough for this trek – it has become something of an obsession. For the last year, every weekend has seen me pulling on my walking boots for treks in the Peak District, alongside a man who has taught me more about endurance than I ever thought possible. As he has planned ever longer and more intricate walks, I have doggedly refused to complain or give in. I have stuck to my determination to do this, just as I have stuck, for too long, to my determination to wring the last possible shreds of happiness from our collapsing relationship. 'You will forget me when you are in Nepal,' he said at our last harrowing meeting. What he meant was he would forget me when I was in Nepal. I do not think I will either forget or forgive. I am all washed-up and glad to have somewhere to go.

To make a new start at 55 is not easy. To lose love at any age is a great loss, to lose it twice over, as Lady Bracknell might have said, seems like carelessness. It is going to be a huge struggle to find the confidence to do anything. Not a good way to start both a physical and mental challenge.

Those endurance walks have, however, had their positive side. They have reawakened my love of the countryside, the open air, physical challenges – many things long suppressed which I realise are important to me. I feel bound, now, for the less travelled road. With a sense of having nothing left to lose, I feel destined to hurtle my way into risky situations. There is some liberation in the thought. By taking risks I hope to live more vividly, even if I cannot live happily.

Since the age of 20, I have been responsible for a family. Finally, last September, my youngest child departed to university and I have been celebrating my 'child-free' state ever since. Much as I love them, I feel my life has been in cold storage. Thirty-five years is a long time to wait to do something for yourself. Now, with no regular employment, a tantalising expression of interest in my writing from Lonely Planet, a fast-track TEFL, a resumed MA in Applied Theatre and a desperate wish to do something more creative, I am about to become a teaching volunteer in Nepal after my trek. My luggage tips the scales as a result, filled with stationery and books donated to the voluntary school for working children where I will be teaching.

The airport staff agree to weigh my luggage in with Mike's, when I explain my voluntary work, and I avoid an excess charge.

My fellow trekkers are a motley crew – I am rather concerned how young and fit they all look. My eyes pan over them as we assemble at Heathrow, looking for a glimpse of grey hair or a beer gut. I am comforted that one man looks like a dedicated smoker. I do not want to be the only straggler. There were to be 38, but the party has shrunk to 35, the three oldest men have dropped out. That, rather alarmingly, means I am not only the oldest woman on this trek, I am nearly the oldest member full stop.

We are introduced to the rep from the Youth Hostel Association who is accompanying us and who looks about eighteen. It suddenly seems very incongruous to be going to one of the poorest countries in the world to raise money for an English charity and I am glad I have the opportunity to stay on for three months and do something to redress the balance.

Most of the trekkers seem surprised I am planning to stay on. I am obviously the first person they have met having a mid-life crisis gap year!

Saturday February 16th

Doha airport, dripping with expensive consumer luxuries seems grotesquely artificial when we change planes in the unnatural 3am glare. I allow myself one item of decadence, a bottle of Bombay Sapphire.

Several hours later I watch with interest and apprehension as our second plane approaches Kathmandu airport, seeing the cluster of doll-like, red-roofed houses set into the hills come into view – my home for the next three months. The dark, deserted airport, a simple, brick building with intricately carved, dark wood windows, seems in keeping with what I expected.

Outside, blinded by the bright afternoon light, a reception committee awaits us with broad smiles. Garlanded with pungent orange marigolds, we are escorted to the coach to a chorus of 'Namaste'– the standard Nepalese greeting. Accompanied with slightly bowed heads, hands clasped together as if in prayer, 'Namaste' literally means 'I salute the God within you,' though one American guide book I have been reading claims it merely means 'thank you.' The same book eulogises the 'happy, simple way of life in the mountains' where girls leave school at ten to help support the family income. I make a mental note to treat what I read with caution and try to be as accurate as I can with my own written observations.

A sign welcomes us to 'The Hindu kingdom of Nepal.' We are driven the short distance into the city, past a seemingly chaotic mix of pastel-washed houses with balconies, crudely made huts and shelters, women in startlingly vivid scarlet and pink saris, small shops with clusters of over-ripe bananas swinging in bunches, small cultivated plots of land – a city swathed in the orange dust and heat of mid afternoon, though my body clock still registers mid morning.

Nepal is 5hours 45 minutes ahead of the UK. I love the quirkiness of the 45 minutes – a bit like the national flag which defies convention by looking as if it has had a triangle cut out of the middle. In no time we are passing the high perimeter fences surrounding the plain, functional Royal

Palace, and entering Thamel where the majority of the tourist hotels are situated, including ours.

Most of the rest of the day is spent acclimatising. I manage to contact Rani, the principal of the school where I am to stay. There has been little e-mail contact up to now. For some reason most of my messages to her have ended in the 'junk mail'!

In return for subsistence I am to teach Drama and English at Shuvatara School and help out with anything else the Principal wants. I am also planning to volunteer for two hours every morning at a school for working children run by the Underprivileged Children's Education Project (UCEP). I have calculated that I should be able to survive for three months before penury forces me home, as long as I live in the local community and not as a tourist.

When we did finally make e-mail contact just before I left the UK, I had difficulty dissuading Rani from bringing a bus-load of children to the airport to meet me. Touched as I was by the offer, it seemed a rather conspicuous gesture in full view of my fellow trekkers.

Repacking my bags makes me a little late for the first briefing about the trek. We are introduced to our trek leaders, Richard, an English guide, and Ram Thapa, a local trekking guide. Ram, we learned later, runs an orphanage for disabled children called *The Hope Centre* in Kathmandu.

120 staff are to be involved in the operation of getting 35 of us up a few mountains (mountains to us, foothills to them) and down again. It seems a disproportionate amount of effort for 35 people until you consider that everything, but everything, we could conceivably need – food, toilet paper, toilet tents, ordinary tents, sleeping bags, clothes, kerosene, cookers, tables, chairs, groundsheets, cooking pots, washing up bowls, plates, cutlery, medicine, drinks, kettles, table cloths (do we need table cloths?) and hurricane lamps – has to be carried with us. There are no roads, let alone shops where we are going, so, for six nights, we must be totally self sufficient.

We are each allocated a kit bag, a red fleece sleeping bag liner and a sleeping bag and told to pack these and everything else we need in the kit bag. I soon find that, with the bedding jammed inside, there is precious little room for anything else. The party is divided into a red and a green team and ribbons issued to attach to our bags to identify us. I am in the red team.

After the briefing, I join the others for a walk through the tiny ribbon of streets around the hotel, but by 8.50pm the shops are closing their shutters – an early curfew due to the outbreak of bomb attacks by the Maoists, so the walk peters out at the famous 'Rum Doodle' bar. 'Rum Doodle' is the alias for Everest (or Sagarmatha as it is known locally) and the beer mats are in the shape of feet. Upstairs, the walls are covered with signatures of famous mountaineers like Sir Edmund Hillary, Sherpa Tensing and Chris Bonington who have scaled the 40,000 (and a 1/2 foot!) peak. Climb to the summit of Everest and you can eat here free for life!

We do not stay long – we are all shattered and I want to be fresh to meet Rani tomorrow. She is sending a car early, to take me to lunch. I will miss the organised coach tour of Kathmandu, but with three months to explore the city this does not bother me too much. By 9.30pm I am in bed sleeping fitfully through the continuous barking of dogs, and it is COLD. I turn on the fire in my room for a short while before I go to bed, and I need to. What will it be like camping in temperatures below zero?

Today was the birthday of a girl in our group and the hotel made a surprise cake for her, which was a nice gesture. I didn't stay for any – I suddenly felt a bit isolated from everyone in the group. I am reminded that today my youngest children will be at their father's birthday party. In another life we might have been celebrating together. Ghosts from the past kept me tossing and turning as much as the drop in temperature.

Sunday 17th February

I wake around 5am and lie staring into space feeling a long way from home. I am tense and apprehensive. I get up and begin re-organising my luggage so that I can deposit a bag of teaching materials and surplus clothes with Rani. I don't want to leave much baggage at the hotel and I certainly want to travel light.

At breakfast I meet two trekkers, a head-teacher and his wife, Colin and Sandra, from North Yorkshire, who have just spent a week in Chitwan at an orphans' settlement. The director of the settlement, Rishi, is with them. They introduce me. It seems I am in for a contrast between the Working Childrens' programme I will be with from 7am to 9am every morning and the private school where I am to be accommodated. Rishi tells me this is a top school where Cabinet Ministers send their children. He seems surprised by my destination but it is a simple twist of fate that I have landed up there, largely due to an introduction from a personal friend of the Principal's living in the UK. Rani was one of the first to respond to my teaching enquiries and, as I understand her husband runs both a hotel and a chain of bakeries and restaurants, I felt I could ask for bed and board without the constraints I would have felt sharing with people of limited means.

I am at the door by 10am when the driver from the school arrives. He speaks little English so I am free, in the back of the car, to absorb the sights and sounds of the city we are driving through. We pass the huge, bleak, featureless expanse of what I later recognise as Ratna Park, the habitué of early morning joggers, meditators and beggars. One section of the park is also an exercise ground for the Royal Nepalese Army. Ahead is the government building. In no time we are crossing the malodorous Bagmati river separating Kathmandu from the city of Lalitpur, and then we are weaving round the pot-holes and bumping over the lumps in the road, dodging dogs and motor bikes, up the tiny lanes thick with orange dust which lead to the school in Sanepa.

I am deposited in the playground. Ahead of me is a small area surrounded by vivid flowers containing a shrine dedicated to Saraswati – the goddess of learning. A ceremony is taking place in front of the shrine because this is the day celebrated as Saraswati's birthday; a day, my guide book informs me, 'for those seeking the power and depth of knowledge'– an auspicious omen.

After a brief chat with a small, quiet man, who is introduced as Niam, one of the Vice-Principals, I am ushered forward to meet Rani, a striking woman in her early fifties, dressed in a formal, dark red sari. She hands me a small, sweet rice ball, from a bowl made of leaves, deposits a small red tikka spot on my forehead and welcomes me to her school. I cannot explain why, but from that moment onwards I feel very much at home.

There is an informal atmosphere here which is very reassuring. The school is a family enterprise run on paternalistic lines – they expect a lot from their employees, but they look after them, house them, feed them and educate their children. Staff are encouraged to regard the school as the central focus of their life. It is clear, as Rani talks to me for the first time, that she encourages people to jump in at the deep end. She responds enthusiastically to some of my tentative ideas. Despite knowing next to nothing about the school, I feel instinctively I can thrive here. I am relieved and eager to start.

We talk about the reports I have read about non-government schools being burned to the ground. I understand that the school has previously been closed due to the political situation, but that things are fairly calm at present. Education in Nepal is a privilege, with as many as 70% of the population illiterate. The school has a strong community programme.

At Rani's suggestion I check my e-mails, then we go to see the accommodation she has arranged for me. Two minutes' walk from the school, set back from the main road, behind a tall brick wall, is a rented house accommodating the school accounts office, an art room and what claims to be, according to the sign outside, a teachers' resource centre, though this has clearly not materialised yet. The building also houses a guard – there is a 24 hour guard on the building, so I am aware that all my visitors will be subject to some scrutiny, though it is comforting to know there is someone else on the premises 24/7.

On the first floor is the art room and a number of very dusty, empty rooms which I am told may shortly house residential students. There is also a kitchen with pink distempered walls, a single calor gas cooking ring, a discoloured sink and an old round table. I am told there is also a small refrigerator currently being repaired. I did not realise at the time what a luxury it is to have even a tiny refrigerator. Along a corridor behind the art room is a bathroom housing the oldest and most cracked plastic bath I had ever seen with a flimsy plastic shower head, a toilet and sink. I make a mental note to buy bathroom cleaner! On the top floor is a comfortable little bed-sitting room with a single bed, a wardrobe, a chair, a desk and an ancient CD-player, which I note with pleasure. Outside is a large flat-roofed area with a table and chairs under a rickety bamboo awning and some washing lines. I will be washing by hand from now on. I will have keys to all three of my rooms to protect my privacy, which is as well because I soon discover Nepalis are inherently curious.

My flat roof offers a view of a number of other houses, with washing drying on the roof terraces and kitchen balconies with metal pots and pans drying in the sun. The household to my left has cultivated the field behind their small house like a small-holding, complete with a solitary cow and circular cow pats stuck in rows to the garden wall.

As we leave we have to dodge round a workman painting the hallway yellow and the guard, who nods solemnly as he opens the large metal gates onto the dusty road.

Retracing our steps back to the school we pass a tiny shack on the corner, with an awning of rusty, corrugated iron. This is to be my ‘corner shop’ where I will buy the occasional egg and soft drinks in the forthcoming weeks to supplement what is to become a predictable diet. The young woman running the tiny store sells little else. She smiles shyly as we pass, a diminutive beauty with huge, bird-like eyes and a very small child clinging to her sari.

We are chauffeur-driven to lunch at one of the family's food chain restaurants and sit out on the roof garden. I am introduced to my first taste of Daal Bhat (a simple vegetable curry with a lentil sauce) and it is a particularly delicious one, as I later discover. We range over many topics to do with the school and talk briefly of our families. Both of us have recently lost our fathers – Rani only six months ago. I found I am missing mine, very, very much. I reflect how envious he would be of my journey – Nepal was one of the few countries he had not visited in a life dedicated to travel.

Rani is much as I anticipated, both in looks and temperament. Short, neatly cut black hair, about five foot four, large expressive eyes and the calm air of authority of someone in an influential position. The formal sari she is wearing is, I discover, because she has an afternoon audience with the King.

Lunch over, Rani has to rush – she is late for the Palace. I assume her invite is linked to today's festival. I wonder whether I will get a glimpse of royalty during my stay, though it is hardly something I have any reason to expect or desire. I am soon to discover that armed guards stop pedestrians walking along the pavement on the same side of the perimeter fence as the Palace. Closely guarded on the outside, the internal assassination of most of the royal family by the crown prince in 2001, sent shock waves through the country. It leads me to wonder if the troops' vigilance may not, possibly, be wrongly directed. However I am soon to discover how the troubles impact on everyday life.

The assassination still disturbs and distresses many Nepalis who venerated the previous king. Conspiracy theories abound as to what really happened, and who was responsible. There appears to be widespread suspicion and concern about the present monarch and more about his son, considered by some a loose cannon, an international playboy and an unsuitable heir to the throne. However, despite these mutterings, the royal family has its defenders.

In what remains of the afternoon I take a stroll down to Thamel's Pilgrim Books, recommended as the best bookshop in Kathmandu. As I walk in, a familiar Tibetan chant bursts from the speakers giving me an uncomfortable sense of déja vu. The bookshop specialises in religious studies, books on the environment, on mountains and on spiritual development. The literature section is sparse and quirky. Dozens of little rooms let off each other with the promise of hours of exploration. There is also a craft section and a café.

Back at the hotel I rejoin the others who have been on an early morning flight over Everest which they say was 'fantastic.' I am unsure whether they are saying that to justify the fact they have all spent about £100 on the trip or because it really was the experience of a lifetime. They say little else about it. Much later in my stay, when I have an opportunity to go myself, it is to prove a disappointment.

Two of the trekkers have visited Ram Thapa's orphanage in Chandol and seem to be in a state of shock over the conditions there. I decide to make a visit after the trek and check it out myself, little guessing what this visit would lead to.

We retire early as we are scheduled to depart at 6am the following morning. I think all of us are apprehensive about what the next six days will bring. There had been much anxious scanning of the paper because of the reported shooting of 126 soldiers by the Maoists in Kathmandu today. This would mean a stepping up of hostilities and ensure a continuation of the Governments' State of Emergency – there is speculation that the action might have been timed deliberately to ensure it. I am told the Government can only call two consecutive periods of a State of Emergency before they have to go to the people, and this will be the second round of three months' red alert. Disbanding the government altogether is another solution for the Hindu monarchy – but that is to come later.

Monday 18th February
Sundarijal - Chisopani

We leave by coach at 6am, past serried ranks of troops obviously on the alert after yesterday's shootings.

By 8am we have arrived in Sundarijal and, with hardly a pause, begin the long, steep climb up a rough stone track. After half an hour everyone is bathed in sweat and a lot of clothes have been shed. All the way up we pass children going down the mountain to the school at the bottom of the pass. There is a fairly steady stream for at least half an hour and the further we journey from Sundarijal the more surprising it becomes still to spot children running down the trail to school. Some Nepali children travel up to three hours every day to attend school. I wonder how many kids in the UK would value their education so highly?

Having said that, there are significant numbers of children in the little farms that we pass who are school age, but clearly working – schooling is not obligatory in Nepal. Some as young as four or five carry babies on their backs. The small houses we pass are covered in a light terracotta wash – an occasional one painted blue or green. As we walk, a fairly continuous army of porters pass us with huge baskets (*docas*) on their backs, secured with wide bands around their foreheads. There are also men carrying drainpipes, mountains of firewood and some burdened down with green shrubs so that they look to all the world like walking bushes – 'cow food' explains my guide.

A tiny child with matted hair stands half-naked by a water tap. A smell of wood smoke and kerosene comes from the house behind him. He watches us pass with big, grave, luminous eyes. Most people we pass greet us with 'Namaste.' One elderly porter in green plimsolls, with a huge load, stops almost as often as I do to get his breath. Already I am experiencing shortness of breath which Ventolin doesn't seem to touch (a corollary of training for this trip was the discovery that I suffer from seasonally-related asthma when I climb uphill). Rees, a huge Welsh guy with a big red beard and an odd, slightly demented laugh, tries out the porter's load for a few hundred yards – that is enough for him to want to relinquish it.

Out of the village we are funnelled into a whole series of what appear to be man-made lanes, carved in the rock, which snake upwards but offer few views. The lunch break is early – 11am. We have reached a big green plateau where a vast army of cooks prepare the food in giant steel bowls – chips, cheese sandwiches, vegetables and juice. It all seems a bit elaborate – couldn't we have managed with a packed lunch to avoid all the peeling of potatoes and boiling of vegetables? The break is a bit long. I have just got into the rhythm of the walk and don't want to stiffen up.

The Green Team, who set off after us, arrive half an hour into our lunch break. The views across the mountains are breathtaking. In the distance, framed against deep blue sky, is a continuous mountain range topped with snow; in the foreground, steep green terraces drop away endlessly like giant steps forged out of the hillside. Scattered down the hill side along the route we have come, we can see tiny farms and lodges perched precariously on the edge of the terraces. The ground is loose and chalky under foot – landslides are commonplace, I am told.

I am in the lead after lunch but soon fall back due to my laboured breathing, but the pace is relaxed and no one hassles me. Small children run ahead of us to shin up giant rhododendron trees and try to exchange the red flowers for a few rupees. Rees accepts them all gravely, apparently unaware they are expecting something in return. His rucksack is soon decorated with dozens of flowers under the disbelieving gaze of clusters of little children. There are white butterfly orchids growing in the rocks. I am glad I am so well prepared for the rigours of the walk. In my head I can hear an insistent voice repeating 'Keep going, keep going.' It is now very hot.

About 2pm we break cover and the view down the mountain is stunning. We are in open countryside now following narrow ridge trails downwards. We can already see the tent encampment below us but it is a steep hour's walk down. We arrive by 3.30pm. I feel I have at least another two hours' walking in me and would rather have travelled further and shortened tomorrow's journey, but maybe this is the best camping spot for some way.

We are in a tiny village called Chisopani, camped on narrow terraces overlooking dozens of distant mountains – the sunset is quite magnificent. The sky seems to burn with a deep orange fire. We are already 2,194 metres above sea level. The levelled ground we are camping on is an emergency helicopter pad and there are a number of these spots in the mountains. We have been told to bring $100 for emergencies so that if we have to be airlifted out we can pay on the spot – the pilots won't pick up unless you can pay up-front and in cash.

I have a thumping headache and a bloated stomach but find myself unable to use the earth latrines – a hole dug in the earth and filled in again after we leave in the morning. We have tea in a mess tent, then retire for a rest. As the odd one out (there are an uneven number), I get a tent to myself and as the trip progresses I am more and more grateful for the extra space – in fact I really don't know how anyone manages two to a tent.

As the night draws in, the temperature falls, and people begin to pile on the layers. A group of pilgrims dressed in dark red and saffron robes passes on the rough road above us with drums, pipes and dancers. There are two small lodges above us and a place to buy water. One or two of us pay a visit to the lodge, not so much for a drink but to surreptitiously use the footpad toilet. As the journey progresses however, we are to find the earth latrines a less malodorous alternative.

Tired by 9pm, after a few desultory conversations with my fellow trekkers, I am in my tent and ready to sleep. The thin mattress supplied is extremely comfortable and I sleep better than I expected – the trick is to keep your hat on. I nestle the camera in the sleeping bag to preserve the batteries from the cold. Tomorrow promises a wonderful sunrise.

Tuesday 19th February
Chisopani - Gul Bhangyang

The day starts damp and cold with a call for 'bed tea' at 6am – black tea pushed through the tent flaps. I take it black, having not adjusted to boiled-milk tea which is how it is normally served in Nepal. The brew is followed a few minutes later by a bowl of warm water for washing. It is important to get the bowl into the tent and used within a few minutes before it goes cold. This involves struggling out of your sleeping bag and stowing it away fairly rapidly so that it doesn't get wet. There is clearly a technique in this.

I manage to wrestle my belongings back into the kit bag in the nick of time because the porters are back to disassemble the tents within twenty minutes. At 6.30 am it is still dark, so there is a lot of fumbling around to find things. Breakfast is a rather bitter porridge, flavourless, very runny honey, more black tea, fried eggs, chapattis and plum jam. The cooks perform miracles producing food for so many so efficiently.

The climb today is stiffly uphill and by the time we reach the top of the first peak, I have dropped behind and the others are out of sight. I am now walking with Lachi, an older Sherpa who walks at the rear of the trek carrying medical supplies. Given my breathing problems we are to see much of each other over the next few days. He stays close at hand throughout my frequent, wheezy stops. We pass through hill villages with cows, goats and chickens, and children who watch our passing with curiosity.

The stone houses have corrugated iron roofs. It is salutary to think that everything apart from the stone and the wood that it takes to build a house has to be lugged up here by humans with the most extraordinary loads carried on their backs, their forehead band taking the strain. There are occasional mules, but I suspect human mules tend to be cheaper and more malleable. We see only one set of mules in six days but hundreds of porters, everything piled up in a seemingly chaotic heap on their backs. Steel bowls, cans of kerosene, kit bags, tents, tables, chairs, dozens of trays of eggs, tinned and fresh fruit, waste bins, metal washing bowls, plates, cups, knives and forks, are all part and parcel of what a trek porter carries.

Some of the porters are well equipped, others walk in flip flops, with flimsy trousers and coats, fine in the strong sunlight, less fine at high altitudes or late in the evening when the temperature falls. Each trekker's kit bag is roped to another and a third kit bag is roped across the top – one porter carries all this on his back. I can barely carry my single kit bag further than a few yards, yet some of the porters are not young and there are a number of women carrying similar loads. They wear vivid cotton or wool bandanas, brightly printed dresses or wrap-over skirts, and plimsolls or flip flops.

By comparison we are elaborately and expensively dressed and I think of the long list of 'essential' or 'recommended' items we have been told to bring. I doubt if our crew have ever owned 'Coolmax' tee shirts or walked in both an inner and outer pair of socks – not that I regret bringing mine – I am just aware of all the equipment the staff manage without, which makes their efforts seem all the more Herculean.

An old lady who looks about 80 – the skin wrinkles prematurely in the sun so it is difficult to put an age to older people – shares a joke with her companions about my walking poles as, sprightly, she hops down the boulders I have just laboriously clambered over. She obviously thinks Europeans complete wimps – I didn't need a translation as she and her friends cackle their way down the mountain.

Most of our walking involves steep climbs up winding mountain passes followed by scrambling down equally steep, dusty paths into the next valley where a new range of peaks emerges. We stop a few miles into the walk because the viewpoint is considered photogenic enough for the 'group photograph.' All 35 trekkers are assembled with a huge YHA banner and photographed in a biting wind against a suitably mountainous backdrop. It seems to take for ever because everyone wants a photograph of the group, so the two group leaders are kept busy pressing a lot of triggers!

Despite their weight load, the porters have reached our next campsite before we have even stopped for lunch. I have fallen back again and manage to lose my footing on a very slippery rock when trying to catch up. My elbow bleeds profusely – 'Oh lady, lady,' says Lachi – dabbing the wound with a none too clean handkerchief.

I finally catch up with the others after a very steep climb. They are relaxing outside a hut, on a rocky outcrop where a large white prayer flag flutters in the breeze, and are preparing to leave as I arrive. The little shack perched on the ledge sells drinks. I hear someone comment on the price. If I had carried a crate of Coke two days' walk into the mountains, I think I would expect to charge three times the normal price. Then there is the problem of all the empties. The ground drops away steeply below us making me appreciate how far we have climbed.

The others are solicitous of my bloody elbow – making me feel like an elderly aunt who needs looking after. Dawn offers to buy me a drink, Andrew dabs an antiseptic wipe on my wound. Then they are off, leaving me with Lachi, but I don't stay and drink in the view for too long; I don't want to fall further behind. So, once more, we set off on a narrow, slippery path precariously close to a sheer drop. It seems strange to see chickens this high up in the mountains and to realise they are from a farm perched on the narrow terrace below.

The peaks rise either side of us in shades of pink, blue and purple; the scenery is spectacular. Cultivated terraces corrugate the lower slopes, red rhododendron trees grow prolifically to great heights below us. More children, blossom-hunting up the trees, attach themselves to us in the hope of some pickings. One little thing has clothes so encrusted with dirt they are stiff and stick out away from his body. As we continue to climb I become aware of how many of the plants are familiar, like sweet scented jasmine, little violets and red berberis. Less familiar are the white butterfly orchids, which grow out of the moss on the trees. The grass is studied with tiny wild flowers and berries. The rock face is chalky and there is a lot of dust.

We climb fairly continuously all morning, until we reach a little building which announces itself as Chipling Primary school. We stop at another hut near the school for drinks. I have caught up again. Then a little further on, there is a lunch stop outside the grounds of a small lodge. It has a view that etches itself on my memory, so wonderful is it in the brilliance of the noon sun, the pathway on the edge of the cliff face and, beyond, an infinity of mountains. They feed us so well, real marching food – fried potatoes, carrots and cauliflower in a white sauce, cheese and onion toasted sandwiches and salad, plenty of seconds, followed by oranges and lemon juice served in a big silver kettle and then tea. I am grateful for the cooked food today, exhilarated and suddenly very happy.

Today was classified as a heavy day and the organisers are not joking – we walk from 8am to 7pm (at least that is the time I arrive) with a short, 45-minute lunch stop plus a few short breaks for drinks. After lunch a lot of the climbing is solitary. I have fallen behind again dogged with breathing problems and a streaming nose. The exhilaration of the lunch stop over, I am suddenly sunk into deep, reflective gloom, probably because I am getting seriously tired. I concentrate on putting one foot in front of the other. I am suddenly aware that I have come off my anti-depressants a bit too soon and that I still need medication to keep my emotions in check. I am glad I am walking alone – I can cry freely. I am not sure I could avoid crying if I was marching ten deep, but at least it saves the others' embarrassment.

We reach a plateau and there is a tiny, isolated, apparently deserted lodge on a ridge. It is called 'The lodge on the edge of the world'. A woman is sitting right on the edge of a man-made terrace as if advertising the name, looking out at the valley below her, a rocky outcrop hundreds of feet below and then beyond that, inky blue in the fading light, the green forests and fields of the valley. I take a photograph, not expecting to do justice to the moment, but in the event it comes out better than expected.

Photo:© Hazel Roy

We are joined on the way down by a young, round-faced Nepali man, the sort who asks where you are from and tells you they have a friend in Nottingham and maybe you know them. I am not in the mood for chit chat, or to be chided because I am stumbling over the words of a Nepali marching song he has decided to teach me. I desperately want to tell him to leave me alone, but at the same time I did not want to seem aloof and unfriendly. I just want to be left with Lachi who seems happy to plod along with me in comfortable silence. Our companion doesn't take the hint. He is with us for another few miles until we descend one peak and climb another.

At the top of the next peak we overtake a little boy at a white Buddhist stupa (a stupa is a small round Buddhist shrine) which we circumnavigate in a traditional clockwise direction. The boy, about six, is carrying a big knife behind his back and the flat edge is making a seat for his tiny sister whom he is carrying on his back. I ask their names and, mercifully, our self-appointed guide floats off.

Our route is laid out in front of us, a long, ribbon-like path snakes down and then up again. On the other side of the next peak is another valley. In that valley are the tents, no doubt with my companions who will, by now, have washed, changed, had a rest and probably their tea. I set my gaze ahead and measure the distance with determination. We stumble into the campsite, already clammy with evening mist, just before the light fails completely, to a round of applause from the rest of the trekkers enjoying a brew and some biscuits. I try to throw off my introspective mood to match their high spirits.

Ram congratulates me and tells me that he now has no doubts that I will finish the trek. Today's walk was obviously a test of stamina and I have passed the test – just. A lot of the group reassure me that they have only been there a short time themselves. I should be feeling a sense of achievement; instead, the applause makes me feel like some decrepit mascot. Tea is prolific – soup, poppadoms, rice and various vegetables, custard pudding, lots of tea. I attack everything with a hunger born out of much exercise.

I talk to Ram for a short time after tea and he tells me about his orphanage. He says he has been 'collecting' children for a few years. It started when he was asked to get involved with the centre, four years ago. The number of children has grown since then as news of the orphanage has spread. Many of the children are disabled and have difficulty finding anyone to house them for that reason. The position of disabled people, as in most other third world countries, is appalling. I try to get him to talk about the Maoists but learn little, though he has tears in his eyes when he talks about the late king.

Ram is a gentle, kindly man but I still felt detached from everyone – not just because I never end up walking with them, and therefore have not bonded with anyone, but because my introspection keeps me separate. On top of the rigours of the walk is an emotional endurance to be managed which makes it feel like a double burden. I give myself a strict talking-to and go to bed shortly after we have eaten.

I want to be in the green-team. They are camped some way away but I can hear Alan, a club singer and comic, regaling them and there is much laughter and song – they are clearly making a night of it. I would join them if I wasn't so weary. My group seem quiet and a bit serious by comparison, made up of a real mix of people; some a bit withdrawn, some a bit cliquey, some very earnest, although I appreciate their many small kindnesses. The group includes a head-teacher and a scout master. In my present mood, I need the comics and not an account of 'latrines I have dug.'

When people are in tents they forget that their voice travels. In the next tent I hear myself being discussed by husband and wife, Colin and Sandra – the couple who have visited Chitwan and who, much later, I am to become great friends with. Sandra thinks I had done ever so well, 'considering.' I am taken aback as we were much of an age!

I do not think being the object of sympathy is doing much for my self-esteem, though I understood they both mean well. Colin has been making reassuring and encouraging remarks to me all day. I feel like a rather backward pupil who needs extra support.

Wednesday 20th February
Gul Bhangyang – Mangengoath

Today, another heavy climb and the news that we might have to turn back on day four as there have been shootings in the area we are due to pass through. Our route takes us through the village of Gul Bhangyang, a timeless place which offers some insight into what life must have been like in the Middle Ages. We stop by a tiny shop on the outskirts selling beautifully carved Nepalese violins (sarangi), small string instruments, which when held and played like one, sound like a ukulele. Alan tries one out and eventually buys one, regaling us with a chorus of George Formby's 'When I'm cleaning windows'; the shop-keeper must think we are a weird lot. Traditionally the instrument is held vertically downwards with the bow moving from side to side like a cello, producing a quite different sound.

We pass what I assume to be a sign for a health centre with midwifery facilities – a drawing in Newari style of a recumbent pregnant woman and a doctor with a stethoscope placed on her bump. I later find it advertises a hospital some distance away.

Today our route takes us through Langtang Country Park. There are supposed to be bear and tigers in the area, but we see only dogs, yaks and mules. We pass the border into the park and make another steep climb, past oak trees cut into strange shapes – the Nepalese cut the branches as they grow. There are many more familiar plants, mahonias, rhododendrons, jasmine, berberis, making me realise how much we take for granted in English gardens. These were almost certainly imported by zealous Victorian botanists.

As we pass out of the lower slopes, the trees fall away and we stop in a clearing for lunch. The sky looks misty and overcast, as if threatening rain. We continue the climb and, suddenly, there is snow nestling in the crevices and a rather silly snow fight ensues. The ground below us is crumbly chalk and shale, and great crevices fall away beneath us.

Half an hour further into the walk and we have as much snow as we could possibly want. The temperature has dropped very suddenly and we find ourselves walking through increasingly deep drifts. It happens so fast that it takes some of our party, who have misguidedly dressed in shorts, by surprise. At the top of a very steep climb is a large stupa with dozens of prayer flags fluttering in the breeze. There is also a lodge which is firmly shut – most of the isolated ones don't open until March. Looking down into the valley ahead is a vista of solid snow, so thick that it is up to our knees in places but, in the distance, I can see the orange outline of tents. By now, though, the party has shrunk to myself, Lachi and Ram who has waited for us.

The main path is so treacherous that any attempt to walk on it guarantees I will land up on my bum. I do slip a couple of times but fear of jarring my back keeps me to the thicker snow on the sides of the path, although when I start sinking into snow up to the top of my thighs, it becomes a bit alarming. Every step is hard won here. It seems to take forever to negotiate the downward slope. By the time I am at the bottom, a welcome party of Colin, and Peter the scoutmaster, have come out to meet me, the last trekker into the camp. I am fairly warm and dry thanks to the clothes I have worn, but some have not been so lucky. Val, who was wearing shorts, has retired to bed with a touch of hypothermia. She is being fed hot drinks and is snuggled up with her metal drinking bottle full of boiling water as a rather effective bed warmer. There are some wry comments along the line that Val, who is carrying an impressive array of alternative medicines, seems to be the one constantly suffering from ailments. She does not reappear till morning.

Everyone layers up with thermals and just about all the clothes they can find. The news is disconcerting. Tomorrow we must turn back. I would have liked to carry on, but have no way of assessing the risks. There is no choice but accept what is decided for the group. I feel very disappointed and retire to bed immediately after tea. I miss a briefing where the group are offered the option of a two and a half hour walk the following day up to the highest summit on the route before retracing their steps back the way we have come.

Thursday 21st February
Mangengoath to near Gul Bhangyang

When I hear about the briefing I have to make a choice – one party is going on, the other back. Those returning include the ailing Val. Much as I want to be included with the intrepid ones, I have to be realistic. An estimated two-hour walk to the summit means a four-hour round trip, even before we begin the walk back to yesterday's site – longer for me at the speed I walk. The return trip downhill doesn't necessarily make it significantly faster because of all the lose shale and the wear and tear on the knees, although I will not have the same breathing problems. If I go, I could face a 14 hour walking day – as it is I have only just got back at dusk on an ordinary day. Sadly I realise it will be impossible. Anyway, I have seen enough snow and am anxious to get down below the snow line.

I set off back with a party that has shrunk to just three; the super-fit have persuaded the others into going on. Val has a stomach upset and the other walker, Aubrey, seems far from fit. For once I am the strongest walker and Lachi and I stay in the lead all the way back. I am glad I have made this choice. The walk back is delightful and, because there is no pressure to keep up, I really enjoy the journey once we have negotiated our way through the snow levels.

We reach the spot where we had eaten lunch the previous day, by 11am, and I am amused to see a party of French trekkers about to enter the cold front in shorts. We warn them what is ahead.

By noon we have arrived at a hill village and I have the leisure to stop for a drink and watch the world of the village go on around me in the blessedly hot sun – women washing under the tap in the centre of the village, chickens clucking in and out of open doors, women winnowing rice in nanglos – large circular flat baskets – sweet corn being stripped off the husks to make popcorn. Bed sheets are spread out to dry on long sticks over huge inclines – if they blew away here they would not be easily rescued!

By 2pm, even with leisurely walking, the tents are in sight. They have been erected next door to a mountain lodge. I have obviously got my timing wrong, but I don't care, I am enjoying my day. The early finish allows me to wash my hair for the first time in several days and rinse out a few clothes. We have not camped here before. Our previous camp site is a further hour's walk ahead, which is why we have arrived so early. That means the following day's walk is a repeat of day two, which was a marathon trek by my standards and will be a real challenge.

Normally, when we get into the site the porters and sherpas have retired to their own quarters, so it is interesting to see them now, the most tiring part of the day over and in the lull before the evening meal preparation starts, taking a break. Some have mats out and are taking a well-deserved siesta; some are chopping vegetables, one or two are having an incredibly thorough strip body and hair wash under the cold water tap. I washed my hair in five minutes – the sherpa before me was under the tap doing his hair for three times as long. They all seem well bonded into a large group – I find myself making a comparison with a wandering circus.

I retire to catch up on my journal and am surprised to see two of the trekkers back at the site by 3pm, positively exulting in the fact that they have been setting the pace for their sherpa. They had passed a sign advertising showers and are off down the hill to take one, before the others arrive. As the showers are solar powered they calculate there will be enough heat for maybe 15 showers (or 40 Nepalese ones they quip). I remember the boy under the tap and pick them up on this. I think of the daily battle to keep clean with all the heat and the dust, with only a cold water tap, with no washing machines, nor any of the other paraphernalia we have to make our lives easier. I think we should be very, very careful about our European assumptions. Who are we to make quips about other people's hygiene?

The three girls from Macclesfield do not arrive for another four hours. They mutter that I have missed nothing – the visibility was awful and we had already seen better views. I am comforted, especially when they say they are totally knackered.

Friday 22nd February
Gul Bhangyang - Chisopani

Something awful has happened to my limbs! I wake aching, insufferably, all over my body but particularly in my knees and ankles. I hobble to the table for breakfast and then try to limber up to get some life moving into my legs, but I am in agony and can hardly move.

I set off on the trek, a twinge in every limb. The route out is up a steep, twisting incline and, within ten minutes, it seems I have not only waved goodbye to everyone in the Red team but most of the Green team too – and they had an uphill walk to get to where we were camping! An hour into the walk and, wincing with every step, I pass Bob, the chain smoker from Sheffield. He is squatting down with his 'tail back' Sherpa, drinking water. 'Dr Livingstone, I presume,' I say. 'Carry on,' he says, 'today I am determined to come in last.' It doesn't last. He passes me eventually with Alan and some of the liveliest trekkers from the Green group, but our paths cross intermittently during the day. They, like me, want to drink it all in and spend time trying to relate to some of the people whose paths we cross – even if it consists largely of mime and smiles.

The path weaves past those marvellous steep terraces which, from a distance resemble corrugated cardboard. The crop here is mustard seed. There are snotty-nosed babies, older kids who haggle for sweeties, women in brightly coloured scarves, babies on their backs and sickles in their hand to cut fodder for the cattle, and others burdened with huge piles of 'cow food.'

Ram and Richard, the English guide, are at a small wayside hill stop when we catch them up. They see me wincing and walking with some difficulty and insist I take Ibuprofen, which I had not brought because I read it can conflict with the Ventolin I take for asthma.

Today, however, the limbs seem more of a problem than the breathing, so I take one and they give me two more for later. They also insist I give Lachi my bag to carry. I have resisted this all through the trek and try to persuade them it is not too heavy, but Richard weighs it in his hands and decides it is. I protest that the porter has already got a bag bigger than mine with all the medical supplies in it, and anyway he has also been helping me down rocks by offering a welcome hand from time to time. Why should he be burdened with my bag now? 'He is a strong man,' they say. I look at Lachi. He is not a young man but he is certainly wiry and strong. I hand over my bag reluctantly and he wears it back to front over his chest. I feel such a failure.

At the next stop the medical kit is called into play again. Behind the lean-to where we have stopped for drinks is a small hut, chokingly dense with grey, aromatic, wood smoke. A small, bare-bottomed child wanders in and out of the door. Ram, who passes this way frequently, shakes the hand of a farmer who comes out to talk to him with what sounds like a real sense of urgency. They disappear into the hut. Ram comes out a few minutes later and calls for the medical kit. He extracts some Paracetamols and gives them to the man.

I want to know what is happening. Ram tells me the man has a 14 year-old daughter who has a fever. The glands either side of her neck are swollen. Ram is no doctor and can only give her Paracetamol to gargle. I ask him how often he is asked for medicine and he says 'frequently.' People in the hill villages have no access to medicine other than the herbs they gather, no antibiotics, not even painkillers. 'Are there any doctors anywhere near here?' I ask. 'The nearest is Kathmandu,' he says. 'What happens if you are seriously ill?' I ask. 'You get better or you die,' is the reply. Other than that you might be able to find someone who could carry you in a basket down to the city, two days' walk away, but then you would need to pay, if not for the hospital treatment, for the drugs. A flight out by helicopter would be financially beyond the wildest dreams of these villagers.

The infant mortality rate is one of the worst in the world – 78.5 per 1000 live births were the figures quoted for Nepal in 1995 by the World Health Organisation. The average life expectancy for women is only 54 – a year younger than I am now, significantly a year less than that given for men.

Since, in the West, women are expected to live considerably longer than men, the low life expectancy of women in SE Asia points to many gender inequalities, in diet, health care and neglect in the first years of life. Women out here get a very raw deal indeed if they are poor and born in the hills.

Reflecting on all this takes my mind off my comparatively minor aches and pains and, by the time I have reached the well-remembered lunch spot, the Ibuprofen has started to kick in and walking is a bit easier. I think I had too long a rest yesterday and that is why my limbs have seized up.

I am the last to arrive for lunch and everyone is about to set off, but the staff summon up some tepid food and, as I start to eat, the rest of the group wave me goodbye. It makes me feel as if I have a contagious disease.

I don't relax for long in case I start to stiffen up again and we are soon on our way. Today is the festival of the family, I am told, and I notice gatherings of family parties at small wayside houses as we trudge along. The trail becomes uncertain now, and we follow a line of arrows, which have been scored in the ground for our benefit.

The last few miles are a real test of endurance. As we descend a wider shale road I suddenly see a motorbike and a truck. The road starts here and we are left in no doubt about that because we are shortly overtaken by the truck, hurtling up the rough road with a cargo of young men clinging onto the back for dear life, forcing us into the side of the bank. After several days away from any traffic it is a deeply unpleasant shock.

I have just recovered when the van hurtles back down again. It repeats the joy ride twice more by which time I am cursing the inventor of the internal combustion engine. We mercifully branch off the road a few hundred yards further along, up a steep vertical track that quite takes my breath away. Over the top and I see there are still some miles to go. My legs have turned to jelly by now. I find myself staggering backwards and forwards over the road. Eventually we pass through the tiny hamlet of Chisopani and within 10 minutes the campsite looms up on the left. It is now very dark and well after 7.30pm. I have been walking almost continuously for nearly 12 hours.

We arrive to the customary handclap. The road to Kathmandu is ahead of us and Ram talks of the possible need to put me in an ambulance the following day – the only transport on the road at present. The Maoists have called a general strike and even the helicopters are not flying. I go to bed vowing I will not accept defeat and borrow Peter's 'Deep Heat,' ignoring my normal deep aversion to the smell. I have not come this far to back off now, or face the ignominy of being carted off in an ambulance. I will never live it down. At the same time I have no idea how I will manage the walk tomorrow.

Tea is an odd mixture. The cooks are clearly using up supplies – poppadums, pilchards, noodles and curried vegetables. Well, it will keep us going. Tomorrow promises a new route, so there is something different to look forward to. The re-routing is because the trek leaders want to finish the trek nearer to the outskirts of Kathmandu. If the worst comes to the worst and there are no buses available, we may have to walk into the capital or camp another night en route. This could be tricky as the majority of the group are due to fly out at 6am on Sunday, the following day.

Saturday 23rd February
Chisopani - Narayanthan

The last day turns out to be so much better than I expected. I wake and the awful shooting pains from yesterday have subsided. I have walked them off! After breakfast, we set out on a familiar track, but within an hour we have swung to the left onto a new, far less travelled, trail which will bring us back within walking distance of Kathmandu.

The walk is through lush woodland; the paths are for the most part level and wide so my breathing problems are minimal. It is absolutely delightful with the sun filtering through the trees, not at all unlike an English woodland walk. There are no villages or lodges or drinks stalls today. We have been told to stock up with water before we leave. Our paths cross with only one other group of walkers all morning. There is little to break the illusion that we are in the middle of England on one of those rare sunny days we occasionally enjoy.

Not only are my legs my own again but I find I am walking with a spring in my step. It still doesn't stop me being the slowest walker but at least I am enjoying the walk. However, I still arrive at the rest stops as every one else is leaving, though I do have a chance to talk to Vicky, a journalist from *The Westmoreland Gazette* in Kendal, Cumbria, who is staying on for another week in Nepal after the trek. The rest of the morning walk passes in tranquillity and shade, free of the ferocity of the sun and the clouds of orange dust that have engulfed us on other days. Advice to bring a scarf to wear as an occasional face mask has proved useful.

It is something of a shock to emerge, eventually, into a wide-open space and to see before us hundreds of fluttering prayer flags. We are in the grounds of a Buddhist nunnery and it is our last lunch break. No one seems to know what will happen when we descend to Narayanthan, several hundred feet below. At present we are happy to sun ourselves in that glow of contentment which comes from a sense of achievement. One by one we slip off our shoes and walk into the cool interior of the temple.

Lunch is served on the grass and then there is a ceremony where all the money we have donated as tips is split up and shared between the crew. 1000 rupees in small notes has been recommended as an appropriate sum by the trek leaders but this seems totally inadequate given the numbers involved. There is obviously a hierarchy; some of the team receive individual envelopes whereas others receive one envelope to share with a group of workers. I try to figure out how far our donations have gone round 120 workers but give up. They cannot be getting more than about 300 rupees each (about £3). Yet the company make quite a thing of it all, asking us to line up and take turns to offer an envelope to each person, in some shabby imitation of Lord and Lady Bountiful. It feels a bit like a school sports day and goes on for just as long. I feel we certainly need to mark the occasion in some way, but not like this. The staff had been quite amazing. We also have a whip round for Ram's orphanage.

Ceremony over, we set off for the final stage of the trek and, en route, pass several scattered envelopes. 'Do you think this is a comment on how much was in them?' I ask one of the others. He is sure it is not. I am not convinced. Everyone has that kind of benign smile on their face of 'having done the right thing by the staff.' I can't help it, I feel uneasy.

We relaxed too soon. The hard work is not over. The route downhill is arduous and hazardous, hundreds of feet to descend, down some of the most precipitous chalk paths of loose shale. Without Lachi I would have broken my neck several times over. Something has snapped inside one of my walking poles – they have just seen me out.

At last we are on the level and there is a couple of miles walk back along a rural road in bright sunshine with corn growing to the left of the road and a small cluster of houses to the right. The mountains we have walked over stand out ink blue in the distance. It reminds me of something Chris, one of the trekkers said when I was standing at the summit of one of these mountains after an exhausting day's walking. 'Look,' he said, taking in the whole distant landscape with a sweep of his hand. 'You should feel proud, just think, we have walked over everything you can see out there, in just one day.' Yes, it was an achievement, maybe not for some, but for me. I am proud I have managed it and am content with that, though I remain ready to do it again if I ever have the chance.

We reach the centre of the village and, to our relief, see two buses in the square decked with large banners across the front saying 'Tourist bus.' We do not have to walk to the city and the others will get home tomorrow, though some, I think, envy my prolonged stay.

I see Lachi standing back on his own. I go and shake his hand and thank him profusely. I see his face clouding. I must give him a more generous tip – he has been such a special help to me. I get on the bus and fish in my money belt to see how much I have. I am reduced to Indian currency but know it is exchangeable. I extract the largest note and go and press it into his hand. Now he is wreathed in smiles.

He waves along with other staff as the buses pull out. It seems strange and luxurious to be sitting down and being driven along at speed and the buses certainly clock it back through deserted roads and streets. The shops are all shuttered securely. There is not a soul on the streets. It is unnerving. Armed troops line the side of the road and stare at us intently. We are stopped once and the soldiers get on the bus but decide we are no great threat and let us carry on. I see the Nepali rep, tense and ready to argue the case as to why the buses are breaking the curfew, but it is not needed. We are dropped at the hotel in less than half an hour, probably a record for that journey. I am sure the drivers are relieved to see the back of us.

Within 15 minutes I am soaking in a hot bath from which I refuse to emerge until my skin had taken on the appearance of a weathered prune. I feel a huge sense of relief and achievement. Then it is down to the bar for the largest gin and tonic I can buy - and another. But I find I have acquired a sort of mascot status as the slowest walker and am plied with drinks by members of the party who I have previously had little chance to talk to. They want to know more about what I am going to do. Mike from Chorley offers to create a group e-mail site to keep us all in touch because many feel they would like to give something back to a country we have all fallen in love with. Well, nearly all of us.

It was some weeks later, when I was talking about the trek to Ram and saying how much we had all enjoyed it despite the hard work, that he told me that there were some that were less than keen. It seems the young YHA rep I had taken as one of the super fit ones, turned back after the first, very easy day on the grounds that the walk was inflaming an old leg injury. So I had more stamina than at least one walker a third of my age! It seemed ironic she was there representing the organisation for whom we were fundraising.

Of course I didn't know this at the time. I just enjoyed the excellent buffet the hotel laid on and the Nepali dancing, applauded along with the rest and retired if not drunk, happily relaxed and relieved that I had survived it all!

Phil, one of the younger members of the party, like most people his age, hadn't yet learned to quit while you are still ahead. He continued to celebrate his achievement into the small hours and then staggered to bed having not packed a thing, with the inevitable consequences.

A New Home

I settle at Shuvatara, A Hindu wedding
I meet the ILO, Orphanage at Chandol, First day of teaching,
Godavari, Pushipatinath and an invite to lunch
Babar Mahal and Rita revisited, WOREC, Art and artists,
A trip to Pokhara, Hol,Holi,Holi, Sunil, Oedipus and the 'grand do'

Sunday 24th February

The first day of my new life, I am woken at 6am to the insistent sound of a coach horn. It seems Phil had crashed out, slept through his 5am alarm call and was still in the Land of Nod at 6am – the time everyone was due to check into the airport. Apparently they had to bring the pass key, shake him roughly awake, and while he dressed, one of the other trekkers had to throw all his clothes into a bag and bundle him onto the bus. Ah, the joys of adolescence!

At breakfast there is only a handful of us. Three of the girls are bound for a week in Chitwan. Vicky from Lancaster and her friend have not yet finalised their plans. Richard, the English trek leader, who is returning to the UK shortly, asks me if it has sunk in yet that this is my home for the next three months. Ram arrives at 10 am and we fix a time for me to visit the orphanage the following week. I need to make a network of contacts if I am to feel at home.

By 10.30 am, having brought some cleaning materials to tackle the filthy bathroom, I am at the door and the car has arrived to whisk me off to Lalitpur. I feel very alone and wonder what I have let myself in for, until I see Rani. She meets me at the door of the administration block clutching a red carnation. 'Welcome to Shuvatara,' she says. There are more carnations in a large vase on the kitchen table and all kinds of basic grocery and cleaning supplies have been brought in for me, plus a lot of household goods. Everything, apart from the new plastic buckets and dustpan and brush, looks well worn, but it is all mine and I am grateful that she has made all these arrangements for someone she barely knows. I now have a (semi) private area I can call my own. She has also brought me an antique copper kettle as a present and we heat it for two cups of tea while we discuss what I might do this week.

Rani wants me to come in and familiarise myself with the school as soon as possible. I had it in mind to recover, sunbathe, swim, do a marathon clothes wash and a bit of sightseeing, but she is my host and I guess all that can wait. I promise to meet her at lunchtime and fill the morning unpacking and doing a lot of hand washing. The number of clothes I have brought are limited and nearly everything warm I have with me is encrusted in dust and dirt from the trek. I attack the grime in the bath. Whoever used this before cannot have been very particular or they had been using it to store cement.

I make a note to search out some tapes and CDs to keep me company. I think I will need them, for much of my time here will be solitary – and that is no bad thing. I decide to treat this positively as a time of retreat, an opportunity to write and discover what I can do, with nothing to distract me. I suddenly realise with a shock that this is the first time in my life I have lived entirely alone. Even without a live-in partner I have always had children around or lodgers, or both. There is a luxury in having a space, however basic, which is my own private corner of the world. I think I could get to like it. I am also aware, that by local standards, it is indeed a luxury.

I meet Rani at the school for lunch in the long, high-ceilinged canteen with windows open to the air and a tin roof. There is a series of long, low sinks to the left for hand washing, as many of the staff, particularly the non-teaching staff, use their right hand to eat with – the left traditionally being used for cleaning yourself. Toilet paper is not something commonly used.

The cooks – universally known as 'didis' (sisters) – all in vivid red saris, give me big toothy grins. The menu, as I discover, varies little. Invariably lunch consists of vegetable curry – usually cauliflower, beans, peas and potatoes with a hot orange relish and a side dish of dhal (lentil) soup which can be eaten separately or poured over the food. There is a meat supplement on some days for those who eat it. Vegetable noodles are served occasionally and about once every two months, chips and burgers (veggie or beef-free, as many of the staff are Hindus) make their appearance, a reminder that the Principal's husband owns Nanglos, a fast-food chain.

Lunch is served from 11am. Left till 1pm when I often feel like eating, the food is past its best. Midway through the afternoon, tea is served, very sweet with boiled milk, plus white bread jam sandwiches. I never get used to the boiled milk, necessary in a country without pasteurising facilities, and continue to take it black when I have a choice.

After lunch I am given a tour of the school. My limbs have started to protest as my body adjusts after its strenuous exertions, and my legs and ankles keep giving way. Rani throws out a supporting hand when I totter for the second time on the uneven roadside and suggests I take more Ibuprofen.

The school has a large complex of buildings spread over a much bigger site than first appreciated. It gives the impression of no central planning – buildings seem to have just been added as the need arises. Newari music floats up from the hall as we go up the outside steps to Rani's first floor office with its wonderful balcony view of the mountains. She inclines her head to an older woman in a sari standing on an apartment balcony opposite. 'My mother-in-law,' she whispers.

A black dog lies exhausted in the sun outside the door to the school office. He adopts the same position for almost the entire three months I am at Shuvatara. He might as well be stuffed. I look across at the slightly flamboyant message on the wall opposite, '*Shuvatara School 12 glorious years of caring,*' and I begin to get a sense of what this means for Rani. The school exudes a sense of family, not just because it is family run – Rani's husband is the Director, her children part-educated here – the school itself is founded in dedication to Rani's mother, Shuva. The atmosphere also has something to do with the age-range and the size of the school.

There are just 600 children here ranging in age from three to eighteen. This seems to make for a warmer and more caring environment than our artificial division at eleven. It offers the opportunity to watch the same child develop from early childhood to adulthood. I am sure it also has the effect of suppressing aggression among older pupils, knowing there are much smaller children looking up to them. I ask Rani if this is the case, and she agrees.

One of the perks for staff is that their children receive a free education here, so a lot of the parents are also staff. Another aspect of life that I like is the sense of hospitality. People are always anxious to know whether you are hungry. 'Have you eaten?' is the invariable opening line to any greeting. Wherever I have worked in England you could die of malnutrition before anyone noticed, or cared, if you were hungry.

One thing I have to get used to, which is a bit confusing, is that in Nepal people incline their heads to the side and shake them from side to side when they mean yes instead of no. What with the language difficulties (my Nepali is currently limited to a few key phrases that I have been practising for my first day of teaching at UCEP – the teaching is in English at Shuvatara), the fact that I talk too fast when I get excited, my problematic hearing, plus the uncertainty this head shake engenders, and communications are likely to be problematic! Luckily a smile goes a long way wherever you are in the world.

In the office I am handed an e-mail from a friend in England – my first greeting from home – it is especially warm and all the more appreciated for that.

Dearest Hazel,
This is just to welcome you to your new school! I hope that you had a safe and exciting journey and that you are having a great adventure. I have been thinking about you and said a special prayer for you this morning.

I know that you are going to have a wonderful time and come back filled with ideas and new projects to go off and do. I miss you greatly but wish you all the best in your new role there. If you need anything or I can do anything just let me know, it's as good as done.

Much love and God Bless, Caroline

The message lifts my spirits. It's great to be reminded that you have friends who love you. I construct a long e-mail about the trek and send it to everyone who has written to me. I consider sending a three word e-mail to my walking 'coach' just to say 'I did it', but decide not to give him that satisfaction.

Monday 25th February - Friday March 1st

The rest of the week passes rapidly. There is a massive electric storm on the Monday night, just after I have pegged out all the clothes I own in the world. They get a good rinse. The lightning and thunder are quite unnerving. I am reminded that this is an earthquake area. I am only relieved that the torrential rain has not started till after the trek was over, as it would have been wretched to camp in such conditions. Everyone assures me this is unusual weather for the time of year. I hope so. The orange dirt roads get flooded very rapidly round here and I soon discover that every time there is a downpour water washes underneath the door leading to the flat roof, so that when I open my bedroom door I have to slosh through several inches of cold, dirty water to get to the stairs.

I also have to get used to the sudden power and water cuts. These, maddeningly, always seem to occur after I have been up since 6am typing inspired copy, which I haven't got around to saving on the computer, or when I have come home hot and sweaty, in desperate need of a shower, to find the tap spits a small venomous burst at me and then dries up completely. The school keeps me so busy the idea of sightseeing gets well and truly shelved.

I set to ordering books – a visit to the school library is a sobering experience it is so poorly stocked – and the cataloguing leaves much to be desired. I found E.H. Carr's excellent *What is History* nestling next to a dog-eared set of Enid Blyton's *Famous Five.* The only connection seemed to be that both authors have first names beginning with the same initial!

Yet this is as good as it gets. Most Nepali children have zero access to libraries. Urged to try some art work and drama with the younger children – I explain I only possess an O level in Art – I come up with an idea for a project on cats inspired by a playlet I find in the school library. It seems suitable for Class One children, until I discover that owning a domestic cat as a pet is a rarity. This illustrates another problem, which is that many of the library books have been produced in the UK or America or Australia, so culturally they are depicting a very different world.

I devise a class on Report Writing for the staff. I go shopping at Ekta Books and come home delighted with a set of *Dr Seuss* books that don't seem too culturally specific. Rani is tickled with them, she has never heard of *Dr Seuss* before. There is no fun in most Nepalese children's books; they are dull, worthy and very, very dry. Education is a serious matter here, but Rani seems happy for me to be creative. At least there is the potential here. She believes education should be fun. On the noticeboards outside are a list of 'smilies' awarded for good behaviour and 'grumpies' for bad.

It's quite a different story when, on Thursday, I manage to visit the school where the working children are based in the shadow of the huge Pushipatinath Hindu temple. I am suitably subdued by the conditions the children are taught in. More of that later. I am due to start there next Wednesday, as Monday and Tuesday are holidays; just as well, it gives me time to think through what I need to do.

I also have a meeting with the other Vice-Principal, Chandreyan, a large man with a booming voice, and representatives from the International Labour Organisation, Bimal and Aditee, to discuss a drama project on child labour.

The idea is to bring together street children rescued by CWIN (Child Workers in Nepal) and children from Shuvatara to research and produce a piece of drama on child labour in Nepal. The aim is to see whether collaborating on a drama project is a useful consciousness-raising exercise for children who will be the legislators of the future. It will be a pioneer project in Nepal and only the fourth of its kind in the world. There will be a Nepali drama coordinator who has yet to be appointed.

The final drama presentation will need to be bi-lingual, in English and Nepali. A month-long sensitisation programme will precede it, which will consist of the children being given a series of lectures on many aspects of child labour. I agree to be involved and offer some suggestions, thinking I have only advisory status. At the time I have the misguided idea that Chandreyan teaches drama (perhaps because of his impressive voice production) and that I will be working with him.

If I had known then that he taught Business Studies, knew nothing whatsoever about drama and nor did most of the kids – moreover, that the bulk of the success or failure of the project would rest on my shoulders, I might have run a mile. The full realisation of what I had taken on came later, by which time I was so committed I couldn't back out if I wanted to. Bimal and Aditee leave lots of material in Nepali and English on child labour and I take some back to my room to begin the background research. It is to be the beginning of a consuming interest as I start to delve into some of the appalling case histories and begin to get a sense of the size of the problem – here is a project for life. It is the dark side of life in Nepal.

On Friday I am summoned to the platform in the main basketball pitch where the children assemble before catching their buses home. Rani is here with a microphone and, before I can stop her, she is introducing 'Hazel Miss' to 600 curious pairs of eyes. I am urged to say a few words so I do, feeling a bit like some visiting dignitary. The illusion continues as 600 children file out, the majority of whom seem to have small floral bouquets to present to me accompanied, in some cases, with hand-drawn cards with the message, 'To our nice new teacher, we are so proud to welcome you to our school.'

I am absolutely bowled over and quite lost for words. I have never had such a reception in my life. By the time they have all gone I feel quite drained from smiling and saying thank you.

I carry armfuls of flowers home with assistance from two of the security guards. It takes an age to find suitable receptacles for them all – I can't bear to leave any of them to wilt and die. I am left with just one mug for tea and a glass for gin and tonic, my nightly and much-needed drink. How on earth am I going to live up to a reception like that?

Rani has decided to give me a weekly expense allowance, even though I am at the school in a volunteer capacity, in order to buy my own breakfasts and snacks, as my stomach rebels against spicy food first thing in the morning. The arrangement is that I eat in school at lunchtime and get a

Tiffin (a large insulated food container with individual metal containers inside) sent round from Rani's house every night. I am happy with this arrangement. I am aware it would be a strain for both of us if I was a guest at her home every evening. When I do accept an invitation to dinner later in the week and we get to know each other a little better, I am aware there are many tensions in Rani's life.

I also meet Rita, Rani's oldest sister, who is living with her sister temporarily. Rita was an actor and TV presenter in her youth but has turned to faith healing since she became a widow. She intends to return shortly and set up a healing centre in the family home near Darjeeling. She is a quiet, delightful woman with an infectious warmth and humour.

Food for the evening meal is prepared, cooked and served by an elderly 'didi.' Her husband is also employed running messages. A number of the school staff double-up as chauffeurs, shoppers and message carriers to the family. No wonder Rani can be so intensely focused on the school. There are no domestic chores to divert her attention. She cannot drive a car. It has never been necessary.

On the sideboard in her drawing-room is a picture of Rani shaking hands with the Duke of Edinburgh. Her school takes part in his scheme, and she met him when he was last in Nepal for an International Conservation Conference which was part organised by my ex partner and his Manchester-based colleagues (one of whom is an adviser to HRH). It's a small world.

Rani talks to me about her son who is giving her the kind of headache most 16 year-olds give their parents but, unlike many young Nepalis, he wants for nothing. He seems to be rebelling against the expectations of highly successful parents who are, at the same time, apprehensive of letting him find his own route. They worry that he is too immature and will go right off the rails. He cannot be allowed to fail – it is too embarrassing for the family if he does not achieve. He has attended a number of highly expensive schools as far afield as Australia, and had private tutors, but is still unsettled and easily distracted. Rani sounds me out as a potential tutor. I am not at all sure I pass the test. Eventually I think she comes to this conclusion too.

I try to reassure his mother that in a few years' time he will be through this stage and will be a normal human being again, but I cannot convince her. There may be other tensions that have contributed to his wilfulness – who am I to advise, knowing so little?

Rani's husband comes home, just before I leave, a short, handsome man who exudes authority. I wonder if his shoulder-length hair suggests the last vestige of a hippie youth? He was born just off Freak Street where the flower children used to congregate in the 60s. Unlike Rani, he has not modified his hair style. She shows me a picture of herself at 16, transformed with waist-length hair. She looks stunning. Sensing my presence creates some awkwardness, I make my excuses and leave.

From family problems and established marriages, to new ones. On Saturday I am invited by Rajan from the working children's school to his cousin's Hindu wedding. 'You'll be bored,' said Rani dismissively – 'Hindu weddings go on for ever.' But I am delighted to have been invited – it is a new experience and a chance to find out more about the traditions of this fascinating country.

Saturday March 2nd
A Hindu wedding

Rajan collects me for the wedding, looking clean and neat – a collar and tie under his leather jacket. I have been at pains to convert trekking clothes into something that looked suitably formal and have ended up in a wrap-around skirt, a long-sleeved T-shirt and a pashmina shawl. It will have to do.

Why I should have thought Rajan would collect me on anything other than a motorbike I do not know. In his early to mid-20s, a car would be well beyond his means. Even a motorbike over here suggests you are doing well. As it turns out, the bike is not his; he has borrowed it.

I ask if he has a helmet and he beams at me, pleased by my consideration. He dons the helmet and pats it happily into place. I explain that I was asking if he had a helmet for me. He frowns, puzzled. 'It is not necessary,' he says. I think of the cows, the potholes and the volume of traffic in central Kathmandu and I think it very bloody necessary, but how to reject his lift in the absence of a helmet? I cannot. I think of all the little kids I have seen flying through the streets wedged between their parents on motorbikes, even the extraordinary sight of a pillion passenger balancing a large sheet of glass on his knees, and I realise I am culturally out of step. I shall have to dice with death too. Getting on the bike and retaining the right degree of cultural modesty is not easy though. Rajan suggests I ride side-saddle. I reject the suggestion. Riding without a helmet is risky enough, riding side-saddle a risk too far.

We fly down into central Kathmandu, weaving through the Saturday traffic with my shawl blowing in the wind. I hope I am not about to do an Isadora Duncan, but despite the risk, I quite enjoy the sensation of flying along in the crisp morning air with all the sights and sounds of the city around me.

Rajan's cousin is the groom and it is to his house in the North of the city that we are heading to meet up with the rest of the family. Plunging down a dirt road we park the bike and walk down the path to his relative's small house. As we get to the door a young woman places a small red tikka spot on each of our foreheads – an auspicious sign. We clasp our hands and bow our heads in greeting, before ascending to the roof where the bride's family are serving sweet, boiled-milk tea and biscuits. I sip the brew sparingly, unused to the sweetness, while I am introduced to several of Rajan's friends and family including his uncle, who works for the Royal Nepal Airlines. I am conspicuous as the only European and feel honoured to be included. Rajan explains that he has dozens of aunts, but in Nepal, as in India and Sri Lanka, you call people 'auntie' whether you are related to them or not.

Later, we walk back down the lane and I get a first glimpse of the bride.

A tiny little bird-like thing, all of 17 years old, very slight and bony with huge eyes, she is dressed in the traditional Hindu wedding attire of scarlet sari with gold trimmings and decked heavily in gold jewellery. She is by the wedding car, which is covered in silver and gold tinsel, garlands of orange marigolds and other flowers.

The guests have a coach laid on and we board it to be driven the few miles to Bankali, near Pushipatinath, where the wedding is to take place. I remember it from the previous week when I had been searching for Sharada School where Rajan's project is based. The guard at the gate was the only one able to direct me. When I eventually found the school it looked as if it had been rotting into the ground for the last hundred years. Maybe it is so much part of the scenery people have forgotten it is there.

Bankali incorporates a (much newer) guest house for pilgrims visiting Pushapatinath and is a heavily subscribed venue for Hindu weddings, which take place in the grounds – there are six taking place today. Beautiful Marquees are erected on either side of the drive, a vivid patchwork of multi-coloured fabrics. As the only white guest I am eyed curiously and with some suspicion by hundreds of milling guests. While we wait for the ceremony to begin I chat to Rajan's uncle about politics and the economy, in a determined effort to comprehend what is happening out here. I am left with only a foggy understanding, but it is unrealistic for me to expect anything other than a guarded response to what may be gauche or highly loaded questions, especially in the current climate.

I want to understand what the ideological differences are between the Nepalese Maoists, the UML (Marxist Leninist) and the other Left parties and factions in Nepal, what their aims are and whether they have similar politics to the Indian Naxilites. The Nepalese Maoists waging guerrilla war in the hills seem to be modelling themselves on traditional Chinese Maoist principles from twenty years back. These include the belief that a revolution will start with the rural peasantry over the issue of land reform and through the generation of resentment against a government that promises more than it delivers.

Increasingly as they gather recruits from the hills – there are claims of coercion to join the ranks – the Maoists are making guerrilla attacks on the urban areas and have declared war on the middle class. From what I have read and understood so far, they are aided and abetted by glaring examples of corruption, nepotism and dishonesty. This is not confined to the elite of Nepal, there is evidence that some foreigners working for so-called 'aid' agencies, seem to think that an adequate qualification for holding down a well-paid job in Nepal is a singular failure to achieve anything back home.

The other thing that comes across is that the country is still destabilised and in shock from the Royal assassinations – the murdered king seems to have been an important stabilising force – but it is so difficult to extract what is really going or to get an overall picture. These conclusions are largely mine, formed from observations and what I have read. Nepalis, unsurprisingly, are on the whole reticent and circumspect in the discussion of their country's politics, I am aware my knowledge is very superficial, I am so new to everything.

The ceremony finally begins. The bride's red veil is lifted by the officiating Brahmin priest, and bride and groom cross hands and are garlanded with flowers. The groom, a young man with a small moustache, wears a taca toupe (the traditional pill box hat) and a grey suit rather than traditional Nepali wear. The bride circles the groom several times, pouring out a continuous trickle of water from a small brass watering can. The formal part completed, the bride and groom sit on raised chairs with their bare feet resting on a support. It is now the turn of relatives and friends to come forward, one by one with presents, but most with an envelope of money. This is received by a man I assume to be the groom's father, who has come to sit next to the groom, depositing each envelope discreetly in a bag at his feet. Each gift giver anoints the couple's feet with water and adds a small addition to the red rice tikka spots on the bride and groom's foreheads.

After about an hour, during which time I have been observing the world go by, I look up at the bride and the expression on her face tells a thousand stories. I think the strain of the ceremony is telling on her. By the time an hour and a half has rolled by, I am beginning to feel really sorry for the young couple – the tikka spots on their foreheads are thick and encrusted with red rice.

Across the driveway, my eye is drawn to a group of young boys, about seven years old, with shaven heads wearing brilliant yellow tunics, taking part in a very different ceremony. They are circling a fire and each one in turn throws on a thin log. Madhev tells me, on enquiry, that the boys are being initiated as Brahmin monks, and the ceremony marks the beginning of their training.

As I watch, I sense someone is looking at me. I turn round to see one of the wedding guests, an elderly lady with a long red line drawn down her central hair parting (denoting her marital status), giving me a look that could turn you to stone. It is both hostile and incredulous.

Unlike Europeans, who tend to drop their eyes when the object of their interest makes eye contact, she continues to stare. Staring is a phenomenon it is necessary to get used to in countries like Nepal where it is not considered rude to gaze intently at anyone who is very different from you, but the nature of this stare is very different. It is a stare designed to intimidate. I began to feel like an alien from another planet.

Next to her is a cluster of young women. One holds a large girl child of about four and I am drawn to the child's eyes which are outlined thickly with black kohl. To me, the effect is vaguely obscene, turning her into a girl-woman. Later I read that kohl is used as a symbol to ward off bad spirits and protect the child from illness. She is quite large to be carried and is wearing the kind of cotton baby bonnet popular in England when I was a child.

Suddenly the child's bladder relaxes, and a stream of urine trickles down the woman's' sari. I wait for the mother to react, but she continues to talk to the woman next to her, while the pee drips off her clothes onto the ground. The girl gets fretful. The mother adjusts her overgrown baby, opens up her blouse, produces a breast, and the child proceeds to suckle.

It is my turn to be absolutely fascinated. It is interesting that in a culture that is hostile to a woman showing her legs – even sleeveless tops can get a second look – a woman can breast-feed in public without getting any reaction. In England I used to get some very odd looks when I breast-fed in public, however discreetly, and once or twice it was suggested that I might like to retire to the lavatory with my child. I also found people back home thought it odd my youngest child was nearly three before she was weaned. This child is much older. It reminds me of a description in *Dervla Murphy's* book on Nepal of the five year old she once saw, unbuttoning his mother's clothes for a suckle shortly before he crossed the road to ask for a light for his cigarette!

Food is being served. The auntie fixing me with the evil eye seems to have had her fill and floated off. I join the queue with Rajan and we are served a range of mouth-watering curries from huge silver dishes. There is also a pudding of sweetmeats and fruit. Unlike English weddings the only drink is water. No chance of getting plastered here then.

A tall, distinguished-looking man in the clothes of the Nepali legislature, navy jacket over white tunic and trousers, joins the wedding party and is greeted warmly by a group of male guests who surround him in the way VIPs always get surrounded. He ignores all the women including the bride. I am told he is someone important in the government.

After about 20 minutes, when he has eaten and is ready to leave, the crowd parts and as he breaks away, he sees me. He makes straight for my chair, extending his hand to shake mine. I am not sure what I have done to be singled out like this. I am dumbstruck, I am the gatecrasher, the interloper, the recipient of drop-dead looks from aunty no. 500. Now this guy, this minister, just because I am the sole European amidst hundreds of Nepalis comes and shakes my hand before he leaves – and he hasn't even acknowledged the bride! When he leaves I am told he is the Minister of Health and I wish I had known. I would have asked him what the government's health plans are for the rural population.

Rajan's two young female cousins seem to have taken to me and want me to stay on for the next stage of the wedding where, so I am told, all the women go back to the bride's house for much singing and dancing. I am not sure what the men do in the meantime. A cluster of women file out of a building in the background carrying ornamental trays of food, including a very large fish on a silver dish. Fish is a special dish in this landlocked country. All the food is covered in bright red cellophane. I am told it is traditional for the bride's family to present offerings of food to the groom's family who will be accepting the new bride into their home. I cannot gauge from Rajan's somewhat ambiguous replies whether this is an arranged marriage. I have not observed any of the interaction you would expect from a couple that know each other well. They have sat detached from one another for nearly two hours, formally making no eye contact whatsoever. Whether this is from reserve or part of the convention that goes with the ceremony I do not know.

We wait at the gates of Bankali for the bus to take the women to the bride's house. The girls suck frozen Kulfi on sticks bought from a street vendor as we watch the monkeys swing from the trees surrounding the temple. The women with the food wait patiently under the blazing sun with their covered plates. Eventually they decide to call a cab before the food spoils.

I decide that maybe I should get back and a friend of Rajan's offers me a lift on another motorbike. In for a penny. As we drive into the lanes leading to Sanepa there is a blaring of horns behind us, not that this is unusual, everyone who drives sounds their horns continuously here, but this time it is for me. A Shuvatara school bus draws up. Already I am getting recognised by the staff, which feels good. I hop on board and wave goodbye. It has been an experience.

Sunday March 3rd:
The orphanage at Chandol

Ram collects me in the morning by cab. The orphanage is on the North side of the city near the ring road where it is semi rural. Down a tiny pot-holed lane is a small building standing in a small field, every inch of which is cultivated. Two steep concrete steps up to the main entrance lead into a dark corridor. On the left is a small office with an old desk, an armchair and a sofa piled high with boxes of chalk.

On the opposite side of the corridor is a room furnished with four beds, which is the girls' dormitory. It also houses Mana Maya, a young disabled woman who cooks for the children, and her baby Sarah. Eight of them share the room, sleeping two to a bed. There are cornhusks strung across the ceiling to dry and the floor is bare, flaking concrete. There are a few basic school primers knocking around and a little rack for their pitifully small array of clothes.

Five share the boy's room. This includes another adult, Bal, with prominent teeth and a lovely fulsome smile, who is physically disabled. He cannot stand upright, the result of contracting polio as a child, and moves around in a permanent squatting position. The kitchen houses a water tap and one calor gas ring. The upstairs leads to an open roof with boxes of chalk drying in the sun – one of their money-raising projects.

The conditions are quite shocking to the western eye – the building looks as if it hasn't had a coat of paint for at least 20 years. The walls are smeared and dirty. I see no bathroom. Their water is drawn up by bucket from the manhole cover in the garden. At the rear of the house there is another little open-air stove for heating water or food, constructed from mud and brick. The children wear a motley assortment of second-hand clothes. They are very shy and either offer me a coy smile or back away a bit.

There is a small charity set up to support the orphanage called the Disabled Children's Welfare Association. They give me a calendar. I agree to return and take photographs of the children the following week to help publicise the orphanage in the UK. I am not sure what to think about the place except to think how unremittingly harsh life is for some children.

At night I find myself thinking about them again. What kind of life will they have? Can we do something to help? I hope so. I have this idea that with my fellow trekkers, I could organise bringing Ram over on a UK speaking tour to make contacts and raise regular funds. I will put the suggestion to him when I have got an email response from the others. July seems like a good time….

Wednesday March 6th
First day of teaching

The previous two days have been busy ones amassing material for my first teaching assignments. Any small gaps have been taken up editing the school magazine, now running to 200 pages and still growing. It will be the size of Gibbons' *The Rise and Fall of the Roman Empire* at this rate. Nima, one of the Sherpas from the trek, has also pursued me for English tuition, but I have managed to put him off till I see the extent of my teaching commitments at the two schools.

The day dawned with my mind ranging over all sorts of unconnected things well before the knock came at 5.30am and before the new alarm clock had time to prove itself. I had asked the guard to give me a wake-up call just in case I overslept – fat chance. I am far too nervous to sleep.

I shiver downstairs to the bathroom, wincing in the morgue-like blue neon light and steel myself for the possibility of a cold shower. Today is a lucky day – it runs hot, eventually. I put on the brass kettle over the calor gas single burner in the kitchen – the trick being to light a candle first, which gives a more reliable flame to ignite the obstinate burner, and then rush upstairs to bundle on the layers. Mornings in Kathmandu start chilly in early March, warm up by 9am and occasionally, like today, end in heavy rain and thunder.

I have planned the day with care. I am to be picked up by cab (I hope) at 6.15am to take me to the Sharada High School. The taxi is at the door when I leave. As we travel through the quiet, early morning lanes I try to plot the eight mile route to Pushapati wondering if I will have the energy that early in the morning to cycle the distance from Sanepa in Lalitpur where Shuvatara school is based, once I have managed to solve the problem of where to hire a workable mountain bike that I can afford. A face mask and helmet seem a good idea too, given the level of dust, diesel fumes and traffic on the roads.

There could not be a bigger contrast between the two schools at which I am to work. Shuvatara has about 600 pupils between the ages of three and eighteen. It is a highly progressive school which encourages innovation and Western teaching methods. The children arrive, well nourished, smartly dressed, transported door to door in canary yellow school buses. Their classrooms buzz with noise and activities. Shuvatara caters for the middle class and upper middle class and is well placed – the Principal is invited to appropriate events at the Palace. Many of the eminent figures in Kathmandu's political and commercial upper echelons send their children here.

'The Formal Programme for Working Children,' run by UCEP, (Underprivileged Children's Education Programme) and financed by UNICEF, is quite another matter. The school runs for just two hours daily, from 7am to 9am, in borrowed school premises. The taxi drops me in the road by the temple, flanked by dozens of flower sellers with the familiar garlands of orange marigolds and other vivid, yellow red and blue floral offerings for the faithful.

The front entrance of the school which I used on my last visit is bolted. 'Where you from?' asks a friendly face in a baseball cap. I tell him. 'Ah, Manchester United,' he says and indicates there is another entrance to the school. I walk down a side road, and try to enter what I take to be a side gate only to find myself stepping into a malodorous latrine. I realise with a sense of shame that the owner must be living in the tiny lean-to corrugated metal shack alongside, squeezed between the back of a bazaar shop and the wall of the school. The stench of urine and wood smoke blends with the sweet pungency of flowers.

The lane narrows amidst a riot of colour, smells, dust and noise and I emerge on a wider street and take the first entrance right into the crumbling white building I take to be the school, through an inner brick paved courtyard and out through another doorway onto waste ground strewn with rubbish. To my left is a set of broken concrete steps and beyond these, the archways of the school building. Under the archway are huddled many sleeping shapes on mattresses covered with dirty quilts and rags. One man berates an unseen enemy and two dogs lope dispiritedly between the sleepers.

Through another entrance and I am in an inner brick courtyard to be met by the stares of a dozen young boys in Karate suits in many different shades of white and off-white, limbering up in the damp, misty, early morning air, in preparation for their pre-school class. They are from the regular school and not part of Rajan's programme. They smirk at me as I stand and watch them while I wait for the others to arrive and unlock the doors to the classrooms.

Above their heads, all around the courtyard, monkeys large and small swing from the drain pipes and patter across the tin roof while the sky shows the pale pink promise of sun through the silhouette of distant cypress trees.

The Karate work-out is in full swing by the time the others arrive and the key to the building is produced. I drag myself reluctantly away from the sight of tiny children bouncing their way athletically into the splits. Inside the dark, dirty, malodorous building, up the well-worn stairs and into the tiny, dark recess that serves as an office, I offload a pile of material and things I hoped might be useful. The children, many dressed carefully in school uniform, file past with shy smiles and greetings of 'Namaste.'

I am offered a school primer and my heart sinks when I flick through the dog-eared, thin pages, devoid of colour and originality. How do children, as young as seven, who may face a gruelling additional ten hours in domestic service, catering or factory work, manage to focus their attention on such uninspiring material? I have brought a cassette tape of children singing the alphabet in the faint hope of there being an electricity supply. My pessimism is confirmed. The school has no electricity and so little light permeates the cramped classrooms; they are more like caves. Children at the back are difficult to see and, owing to their subdued little voices, difficult to hear too. The most sophisticated resource is the blackboard and small chips of chalk. I enter the first class accompanied by Rajan, feeling as if I have just gone 'over the top' into battle.

I invest much energy into the first hour and things don't go too badly, though with thirty-three in the class we don't get much further than exchanging basic information, (*Mero nam Hazel ho* – my name is Hazel), asking their names, (*Tapiko nam key ho?*), getting them to reply in English and asking them to write their names on the blackboard board. I sense the pupils are rarely picked out individually. They recite the alphabet monotonously to prove they know it, though few know how many letters there are; they are learning by rote. We go through numbers one to twelve, they write them down and I tell them that tomorrow we will look at telling the time in English. Rajan, my translator, brusquely repeats the information to some small children who do not appear to have understood my simple instructions.

Three children appear with marigold garlands in their arms and I am ritually adorned and have small floral offerings pressed into my hand. I feel so embarrassed. What do they expect of their 'guest' teacher? Can I really fulfil a fraction of their expectations?

I enter the next class. Running alongside my dark, cramped classroom is an open balcony. Why aren't we out in the light – or is the balcony unsafe? This class is a big challenge – the children cover classes 4-7. There are 45 of them. There is no way I can assess all their varying levels of ability in 40 minutes. I am determined to catch all their names so we go through a quicker version of 'my name is' and Rajan writes the names on the board. Many appear unfamiliar to him. I ask him afterwards if he has a record of all the pupils' names. He says he does, but it is obvious the children are not used to being identified individually. Many are more used to being called by a generic name like 'kanchi' (little sister), which is commonly used for domestic servants. This is a long way from modern child-centred teaching, but has echoes in my memory of the grim, post-war primary school I attended nearly 50 years ago, where it took the teacher two years to realise that I could not read, because there were 59 in the class.

Faced with the impossible task of finding a common level with so many children in such a short time, I fall back on the section of the primer I am told they have reached. We go through the difference between big and small, high and low and tall and short. I try to move onto 'big, bigger, biggest', 'small, smaller, smallest', but it is all a bit much for them. I soon realise only five or six of them have the book.

I have overrun by 15 mins and missed the Shuvatara school bus which has a pick-up point near Pushipatinath. Rajan walks me up to the main road. I ask him about a very tiny girl who has had difficulty keeping up in the first class. He says she is seven and in domestic service. She looks about four years old in size and stature.

I get Rajan to hail a cab, explain where I need to go and to negotiate me a reasonable fare. As we pull away the taxi driver yells '200 rupees' exultantly. We haggle a bit, as it cost me half this amount to get here. 'You are English' he says – 'have lots of money.' I tell him that it costs 10 times more to live in England and translate the cost of food back home into rupees. He still can't get his head round the notion of relative poverty and who can blame him? By their standards I do live in princely luxury even without a regular income. Later I am somewhat ashamed of myself when I realise I have been haggling over £1 for a journey of several miles.

Back at Shuvatara, the children are playing happily in the airy, large playgrounds in their bright-red baseball jackets. 'Morning, miss,' they say with a grin as I pass. They are self-confident, outgoing, with a school day, a proper lunch, and a home to go to at the end of the day, a home where they will be treated like children and not cheap labour. Some, I suspect, may come from families employing children the same age as their own, as domestic servants.

I bump into Rani and tell her about my morning. She immediately offers to help and stops a hulking great lad who looks like a baseball player, ostensibly to ask about his university applications, but also swiftly commandeers him to assist me. I love her style. I try to explain to my new assistant, Sovhit, what the school is like, and he agrees to meet me there at 7am tomorrow. I e-mail Rajan to tell him I have help, and ask him to send Rani details about UCEP.

I have a project on cats with class 1A. I find the children's English vocabulary is very good – they know the difference between carnivores and herbivores, they know what a mammal is and they are quick and happy to respond. I discover dogs far outweigh cats as household animals of choice, probably because they are acquired as guard dogs. Animals generally are not treated as pets. One little girl tells me quite dispassionately that her dog killed a neighbour's cat because 'he does not like them.'

In the last ten minutes, because they are getting a bit restless, I ask them to draw me a cat – any cat, and they come in the shape of lions, panthers and multi-hued domestic cats. I read them the little play about cats and tell them we will make puppets and masks next week so we can act the play out. They are clearly used to learning creatively. I send them home with a list of junk items to collect for next week. I plan to repeat the lesson plan with 1B and 1C on Thursday and Friday respectively. Despite all the cultural differences there is enough familiarity for me to feel confident at Shuvatara, while at UCEP I am overcome with the enormity of what I am trying to undertake.

I go home to rest an upset stomach, an inevitable and regular side-effect of living here, however careful you try to be. A sudden power cut at 10.00pm leaves me grateful I have just saved my work on the computer. I retire to bed with a torch.

Thursday March 7th

Breakfast this morning is a cup of black tea and a glass of water as I am still suffering from vicious stomach gripes. I time it better this morning and the cab arrives at the temple at 6.55am. By now I have the route sussed. The sky is overcast. It has rained again heavily in the night.

I go through the back entrance into the school – there is a heavy mist again this morning and the itinerant sleepers have made a fire by the doorway. Their clothes are encrusted with filth in stark contrast to the children who stream past in their neat blue uniforms.

Sovhit turns out to be very useful. Throughout the day we make a series of discoveries – many really don't understand English, some don't even know how old they are; I form the impression the classrooms have not been cleaned since the building went up a century or so ago and I am told the children are unusually quiet with me because they are still shy, though in some cases this could be because they work long hours and get little sleep.

In one class I have 47 pupils between the age of 9 and 25. Our lesson plan involves 'telling the time' and I explain we will make clocks from paper plates tomorrow. Sovhit suggests they make them at home (what is 'home' for most of them?) but I point out they are unlikely to have the time or resources to do so and that if we want them to do this we will have to supply the materials and make them in class.

I ask Rajan for some of the supplies I have donated to the school and distribute pencils, pens and pencil sharpeners today – I suspect they may be kept under lock and key otherwise. Rajan wants photographs of me handing over biros, which seems a bit excessive, but I oblige reluctantly.

At the end of the school morning it is clear Sovhit is undeterred by the conditions at Sharada. He talks of getting Shuvatara to donate exercise books and of recruiting additional pupils from the school to help.

Ashok, who seems to fulfil a multiplicity of functions, arrives to take me bicycle hunting at 5.30pm. This involves a pretty hairy motor bike ride to downtown Lalitpur. I tell him that in England all pillion passengers have to wear helmets but, like Rajan, he informs me, airily, that they are 'not necessary.' 'In that case why do the drivers have them?' seems the obvious retort.

The bikes in the shop looked terribly crusty and the shop keeper looks puzzled when I ask if they have a woman's saddle, which is not surprising when so few women ride bikes. The ancient ones I try out creak, groan and squeal. Ashok gets the hire price down to 3000 rupees for 10 weeks but with new ones priced at 6,000 rupees that doesn't seem too good a deal. I say I'd like to try the hire centre for Himalayan mountain bikes the following day.

Just as I am settling down for another quiet evening, Nima the Sherpa arrives. He has travelled over from the far side of Kathmandu by bike – a rather better one than those I have been looking at! He wants English lessons every night at 6pm before he goes on a trek to Annapurna. I agree to give him three classes a week. I ask if, in return, he will suggest some trips out for me, which he can write up in English as his first assignment, as well as helping me with my Nepali.

Rani phones to say she is sending over rice and yoghurt for my delicate constitution and two CDs. I wish someone would send a replacement fire as it's pretty chilly up here (the previous one had to be returned when it turned out to be electrically lethal). The yoghurt arrives – it is delicious but I pass on the 'Greatest Love Hits' CDs – not really right for my current state of mind.

Friday March 8th
(International Women's Day)

I am already awake drifting over all kinds of things when the alarm bleats like a sick sheep. I am outside before the cab driver this morning, but the security man rouses him. I hadn't realised the driver lived next door. He now trusts me to give him the regular fare each trip so today the meter is switched off and, not surprisingly, we go a quicker and quieter route.

Today Amrit is there, but not Rajan. Apparently it is an official holiday. No one has told me, but since two thirds of the students turn up anyway, along with Sovhit, my sterling helper, we are still gainfully employed. I am told we do not have to stick to any kind of lesson plan since the groups has 'finished' their English courses for the term. I don't know how this is assessed, since many of the pupils don't appear to understand any English at all. Still, if this is a holiday, we should celebrate the right to play – it is clear these kids get little enough of that!

Today, within the context of 'telling the time' we learn more about the pupils' lives. A few rise as early as 4 or 4.30am, the majority between 5 and 6am. Most work an irregular number of hours – a ten hour working day is not unusual on top of the two hours they spend at the morning school. Some point out they have to work before they come to school at 7am. The majority have finished work by 7.30pm but a few were still working at 10.30 or 11pm.

The vast majority are domestic servants working in private houses. Four pupils work in a shop, two have jobs as domestics as well as working in a restaurant. Two girls in their 20s work in a carpet factory.

Since both lots of pupils are pretty bored by the time we finish our brief survey, I attempt to teach them *'What's the time Mr Wolf'* for some light relief. There is much hilarity as we play it in the corridor – Amrit comes along after the first session to find out what the noise is all about and stays to listen with a wry grin on his face.

Several times I think the tin roof is about to collapse as heavyweight monkeys hurtle over our heads. The children screech with mock fear as each new wave of monkeys pound across – there are a lot this morning – devotees at the temple feed them, so they have been a fixture here for years.

As we leave I discover that I am expected to work on Sunday. Most Nepalis work a 6-day week, with Saturdays the day of recreation, but since I am tutoring on Saturdays I request Sundays off. It is to be a few weeks before I adjust to working six days a week.

On the school bus Sovhit tells me about his family. His father works in a department store in California. He sends money home to support the family. He has not seen his father for four years.

While I am waiting for a meeting with Rani, the editor of the ever-growing school magazine enlists my help again, and I read a horrifying article (strange topic for a school magazine) about a 14 year old girl who was raped by the brother of her sister-in-law (in Nepal you can be made to marry a man who rapes you). The bastard made her pregnant. Some of her relatives arranged an illegal abortion.[1] The sister-in-law betrayed her to the police. The rapist was released in court and the woman was jailed for 20 years.

I can hardly believe what I am reading. I have to ask for verification. Yes, I am told, it is true, and though the normal legal sentence for this 'crime' is three years, in reality women serve much longer sentences which often means children are jailed with their mothers because there is no one else to look after them.

Something like 20% of all women in jail are there for aborting a foetus and there are graphic descriptions of some of the horrendous lengths women go to, to abort, including piling tons of rocks onto their stomachs and inserting sharpened wooden sticks into their cervix – a frequent cause of death. Since hospital treatment costs nearly two-thirds of the average

1. In 2002 the Nepal Government finally passed a liberal Abortion law after three decades of reform efforts, but the first Government Abortion Services did not officially begin till March 2004.

monthly salary, few women abort using a qualified doctor and even where this is the case, doctors have little experience of this medical procedure so treatment frequently goes dreadfully wrong, even in hospital.

We discuss the situation in the UK by contrast, and the changes in attitude towards both abortion and illegitimacy during the last 30 - 40 years. I am asked for my religious views and explain that I was reared as a heathen, though I had a short flirtation with the Anglican Church when I was young. I express my sense of outrage with what I have just read and offer the opinion that the wrong person was punished and that the bastard who raped her should have had his balls cut off. My companion seems both amused and in tacit agreement with this forthright response from this mad white woman, which is in stark contrast to the quiet restraint of the average Nepali.

Class 1C's cat project goes quite well today, though I have difficulty understanding the children; their accent, plus the speed with which they speak, coupled with the quietness of their voices, is pretty challenging for someone with poor hearing. I am offered handfuls of honeysuckle they have pulled from the bushes around the school playground. I am not sure Rani would approve!

By 12.40pm, I am in the packed Hall along with all the upper school for the first of the sensitisation programmes on child labour with the ILO representatives. It is introduced by Bimal.

The dispassionate account of child labour with supporting slides and video is pretty devastating. These are some of the statistics we are given:- In 1996, 29.1% of the total child population of Nepal were involved in child labour (census figs for 2001 were not yet available). 800 million adults are unemployed whereas 250 million children work. The Global Distribution of Child Labour breaks down as follows:-

7% Latin America and Caribbean (17,500,000)
32% Africa (80,000,000)
61% Asia and Oceania (153,000,000)

Of a child population in Nepal of 6,225,000 there are 2,596,000 working, 1,660,000 are economically active (employed full time). Waged child labour accounts for 279,000. The worst forms of Child labour account for 127,000. Latest figures show that of 7.9 million children up to the age of 16 in Nepal, 2.5million are working – nearly 25%.

Schooling only	**Working** Irrespective of school attendance	**Idle** Or not stated	**Working and schooling**	**working only**
2,287,000 (36.7%)	2,596,000 (41.6%)	1,324,200 (21.7%)	1,587,000 (25.5%)	1,004,000 (16.1%)

The worst forms of labour in Nepal include Porters, Rag Pickers, Prostitutes, Children in Bonded Labour and Domestic Servants (a comment is made that some of the pupils in the audience probably have children of their own age in domestic service in their houses)

The ILO Convention No 182 (Article 3) Outlaws:-

- *All forms of slavery or practices similar to slavery, such as the sale and trafficking of children, debt bondage and serfdom, forced or compulsory recruitment of children for use in armed conflict*
- *The use procurement or offering of a child for prostitution, production of pornography or pornographic performances.*
- *The use procurement or offering of a child for illicit activities, in particular for the production and trafficking of drugs*
- *Work which by its nature or the circumstances in which it is carried out, is likely to harm the health, safety or morals of children*

We are then given the following information about the SCREAM Project:-
ILO/IPEC(International programme on the Elimination of Child Labour) have developed a project entitled SCREAM (Supporting Children's Rights through Education, the Arts and the Media) as a means of entertainment, and to apprise the civil society on the ramifications of child labour.

IPEC Nepal, complementing the global campaign against child labour, joined SCREAM as a pilot country in 2001.

IPEC Nepal, under SCREAM, aims to contribute towards developing networks of young people and educators, to involving the media and to integrate into our work the theatre, literary and artistic communities. Theatre and alternative media play a powerful and influential role in portraying social and cultural life, as well as social injustice such as child labour, that exists in society.

Theatre in all its forms, acts as a popular medium to educate, inform and entertain the general public on social problems. Theatre is an excellent learning method for children and young people, combining fun and entertainment with a means to develop confidence, memory, self-discipline and self-esteem.

There is little response from the floor. Bimal impresses me greatly. He concludes with a story about a great hurricane that devastated a large area. Thousands of fish were hurled inland in a terrible storm and left floundering on a beach. One man stood there throwing the gasping fish back in the ocean. 'You're mad,' said an observer. 'Why are you doing this? You can't hope to rescue all these fish.' The man looked at the fish in his hand and said, 'No, but I can make a difference to this one.'

Chandreyan whispers to me, 'Do you wish to say something?' I hadn't anything planned but I get to my feet and tell the audience that I frequently want to right wrongs, but usually feel powerless to do anything. I remind them of the fish story. I say, 'We maybe cannot shift mountains but one step forward is worth making and for once we have been handed a way of making a difference – so let's use it!' I hope it strikes a chord. We will only find out in the next few weeks. I doubt if all the children will want to be involved – it will be interesting to see what happens now.

Having collected the ILO fact sheets, I hitch a lift to the Himalayan mountain bike warehouse on a school bus going to Lazinpath. With the help of Geoff, an Australian, and Hari, within 5 minutes I have a bike – it fits me, it rides like a dream, it has front suspension and I want it. I agree to buy it for $250 (about £195) and they agree to buy it back in May for $150. I follow Hari back to a small outlet in Thamel and get kitted out with a helmet and padlock and withdraw 19,500 rupees from a hole-in-the-wall at the Kathmandu Guest House, probably to the shock of my bank manager. I suppose I could deny doing so, since the bank told me there was no ATM facilities in Nepal!

The ride back from Thamel starts well – what a difference a good bike makes. I have just convinced myself that despite the horrific build up of traffic all around me I am OK, because the traffic seemed to weave round the bikes, when there is a squeal of brakes and, just ahead of me, a young lad is knocked off his bicycle by a motorbike and then the biker just buggers off.

What a bastard! I look at the kid. His bicycle is old and battered and he is poorly dressed. Maybe he is one of the domestic 'slaves' we have been discussing today. Is this why the motor biker feels it OK to abandon him to his fate? He has limped back onto the central reservation pulling his bike behind him, but one of his sandals has been left at the mercy of the traffic in the centre of this huge roundabout. I am on one side of the road, he is on the other, but I am determined to get to that cheap plastic sandal before it is crushed under the wheel of a car.

I wait ages and so does the kid – well he doesn't have a choice. Buses and lorries continue to weave around the shoe, barely missing it. Any minute now it will be crushed. In the merest gap in the traffic, I plunge into the centre of the road, holding up one hand imperiously, and manage to scoop up the sandal and hand it to its owner, before the traffic closes in again. I feel so angry about the way everyone has ignored this kid, and then I think what a funny spectacle I must seem to him, this fiery, middle-aged white woman with a strange purple plastic helmet on her head, who has just held up the traffic at the height of the Kathmandu rush hour. I get on my bike and cycle away.

Photo: © Hazel Roy

Saturday March 9th
The Hope Centre re-visited

Ram calls for me at 9am to take me out to the orphanage to photograph the children. I walk out of the gate to wait for him only to step back smartly as a long line of troops walk silently past with cocked rifles. 'What are they doing?' I ask the security man. 'Practising,' he says.

The weather has changed perceptibly in the last day or so. It is a stunning, hot clear day. I feel I have made the adjustment. The first visit I made to the orphanage I was shocked by the conditions the children live in. Today they are out in their large sunny garden and everything seems that bit better. Ram tells me to take my time photographing them because I want some natural shots and they are clearly self-conscious and shy around the camera, particularly Nirmala, a striking-looking girl with only one leg – she lost her other one in a road accident that killed both her parents.

Gradually they relax and I try to take photos of them as surreptitiously as possible. I have written some copy about the centre after my first visit

Photo: © Hazel Roy

and e-mailed it to Ram and after this visit I am able to amend it and include some new information. Basanta, the eldest boy, has been away several days attending the funeral of his aunt, his last living relative. When he arrives back, he can barely keep awake. The journey back from his village has been long and gruelling, particularly for someone with a chest and spinal deformity.

Ram and his colleague are deep in conversation planning how to pump water from the stream at the bottom of a steep incline up several hundred feet to irrigate their crops, and how best to terrace the land which slopes down to the stream.

At a corner of the house, water is being boiled in a battered tin container on a small, makeshift stove over a small wood fire. Two girls strip the baby Sarah, oil her hair and redress her. Mana Maya, the baby's mother, lost her leg in a landslide accident that killed her entire family and left her destitute and three months pregnant. She helps with the cooking at the centre. Bal, the other adult, gives me his lovely toothy grin. Despite no use of his lower limbs he levers himself around the centre by his arms, at quite a speed.

While I am waiting for Basanta to return I am invited to lunch. I manage to get some of the girls to thaw out by going through their English primer with them in their bedroom. Hanging over our heads is the chain of dried sweetcorn pods encased in their husks from an earlier harvest, which I remember from my last visit.

Ram talks about his hope that some of the boys will be able to join him in the trekking business and some of the girls will be able to help out in the office. A former teacher, he has many plans to make them self-sufficient and provide a decent education and training for all his 'family'. Later, at home, I rework the article to send to my fellow trekkers:-

Travelling Hopefully

Ram Thapa has a double life. He is a trek guide leader, and a very good one at that. I first meet him in this capacity when I undertook the Helambu circuit trek in late February 2002 – one of 35 trekkers who had taken up the YHA Nepal challenge to raise £2,000 each for the Youth Hostel Association.

I think I can speak for the other trekkers when I say that, as the days passed, we not only gained in admiration at the stamina and hard work of the trek team led by Ram, but also the ingenuity, fortitude and diligence of the Nepalese hill people, whose lives are an unremittingly hard struggle for survival. Many of us felt we did not want to leave this unforgettably beautiful country without offering something back and Ram's other life gives us an opportunity to offer some practical help.

For Ram, when he is not scaling mountains and looking after the numerous needs and demands of trekkers, runs a small orphanage in the Chandol district of Kathmandu, which is presently home to 13 young people who have lost parents, or have parents unable to support them. A number have physical disabilities – some have conditions that might respond well to appropriate medical treatment – if this could be afforded. I visited the orphanage the week after the trek and met the children.

Basanta Shakota, 15 years, is tiny for his age and suffers from a bone deformity to the upper chest. He has been at the centre for a month, since the death of his uncle – the last of his living relatives able to offer him a home. Anita and Bimala Lama are sisters, 12 and 10. Like brother and sister Keepa (8) and Migma Sherpa (5) they have been at the orphanage since it opened 4 years ago. Keepa has a metal plate in one leg due to a road accident and has great difficulty walking. Then there's Sumitra and Nirmala (both 11) – Nirmala has one leg and walks with crutches, Serkj (7) Umesh (6 and partially disabled) Passang (5) and the three Raimajhi children, Sumitra (7) who has a sight problem, Sujit (4) and Gayatri (6), who have been with Ram for 3 months. Their parents were tragically killed three months ago in the crossfire between the Royal Nepal Army and Maoist troops in their home district of Mugu, and no other relative could afford to take over the care of the orphaned family.

Finally there is little Sarah Poudel, just two and a half. Her mother is physically disabled due to a landslide accident that killed her husband, mother and father and left her with only one leg, three months pregnant and without any financial means of support. She lives at the centre too and cooks for the children. 'They are my family,' Ram says, simply.

The orphanage has tiny, rented premises, with a single bedroom for the girls and Sarah's mother and one for the boys. Furniture is sparse and some children have to share beds. Ram take turns with a small group of other supporters to sleep in and look after the children. Their small organisation, The Disabled Welfare Association, calls the building The Hope Centre and there is a committee of nine who do their best to raise the running costs of £300 per month to feed and clothe the children. The land surrounding the building is tilled and crops are sown on every inch of the land to help provide food for the children. On the flat roof there is a tray of chalk drying in the air. The children make boxes of chalk that are sold for 9 rupees a box – about 9p – to supplement their income – they sell what they can to local schools. All the children attend a local school and a blackboard in the boys' bedroom evidences the beginnings of the ABC with examples in English. There is no free medical provision – you choose between free hospital treatment where you pay for the drugs, or a visit to a doctor who charges a fee that includes medication. Doctors charge 2-500 rupees a visit. Of the £3,600 that needs to be raised each year to provide these children with their basic home, only 50% is currently secured by donations from local charities or individuals donating abroad. As well as money, the children urgently need clothes and more bedding – there is insufficient room in the cramped building for more beds.

If we could donate between us the cost of bringing Ram to England on a fundraising tour, and all those who could, put him up for a few days and introduced him to local schools and businesses in their area who might be able to financially support the project, Ram could return with a network of financial supporters who could provide some stability for the orphanage for the first time in its four years of existence. There are many children in Nepal who need help. We could make a difference to a few of them.

Hazel Roy

Photo: © Hazel Roy

Children from the Hope Centre. Photo: © Hazel Roy

Another world from the Hope Centre…
Back in Sanepa the heat is intense so I decide to go for a swim. The local Aroma Sports Club has a swimming pool and offers facilities to Shuvatara. The pool is deserted when I arrive, apart from a couple playing tennis and a lone white woman, in a leopard skin bikini, stretched out on a lounger, while three young blonde children play at her feet.

She does not acknowledge me, even when I let out an involuntary gasp as the iciness of the water hits me – it feels as if it has been pumped there from the top of Everest. In water this cold I can only manage 2 lengths before going numb all over. That explains the deserted pool! The couple finish their tennis match, and the woman by the pool packs up and joins them. They drive off in a chauffeur-driven jeep without a backward glance.

In the early evening I try out my bike on the unfamiliar local lanes, my nose anticipating the large, rotting heaps of rubbish dumped at the junction of the roads well before my eyes catch sight of them in the dusk. They are being picked over by local dogs, cows, or the occasional bare-foot child. I discover the British school in the locality and several more local shops before heading back. The lanes are for the most part unlit and I have no lights, not anticipating I would use the bike after dark.

Sunday March 10th
Godavari

Up early to enjoy my day off, I resolve to get out of the dust of the city, and walk the two miles into Patan. My route to the bus station takes me through a fascinating, centuries-old, shopping street thronged with early-morning crowds. Shops selling brass bells and religious statues compete with basket weavers, ironmongers selling pots and pans, fabric shops selling bedspreads and saris, market stalls selling saffron and loose tea, and outdoor shops selling cheap coats and rucksacks. One part of me wants to be up in the hills and out of the city's noise and dust, the other part of me revels in all the sights and sounds of this wonderful thoroughfare – Sunday is a busy shopping day after Saturday's closure.

The street opens out onto Patan's Durbar Square, with its fascinating array of centuries' old temples. They deserve a day's exploration in their own right. Beyond the Square is Langarkhot Bus Station. I find a micro-bus going to Godavari, but when I peer inside there appears space for only an undersized 5 year old. I hesitate one second too long, for two adults push past me and achieve the impossible. Fighting through the tangled limbs they find somewhere to sit inside this oversize wardrobe on wheels. The heat emanating from the bus is stifling; I elect to wait for the next one and enjoy the bonus of a window seat. We share this bus with a couple, obviously retiling their bathroom, as the van is loaded down with 15 boxes of tiles, over which everyone has to scramble to get a seat. I sit behind a little baby with huge eyes and the snottiest of noses, which I want desperately to wipe, but fear offending his granny by doing so.

The bus weaves uphill out of Patan. To the right are fields of mustard, a riot of yellow, and in the valley the vivid green of rice paddy fields. As the road bends round, two chimneys are etched in the background belching out fumes. It is the local brick works. I am reminded of the cover photograph on a book on child labourers I am reading, which shows a line of kids, between the ages of 7 and 12 (they could be older – child labourers are small for their age), stripped to the waist carrying piles of bricks on their head – some as many as ten. I recall the story of Surya, 14, who makes 500 bricks a day for 70 rupees, working from 4am to 7pm, who longs to return to the hills. He will be able to take back little to his widowed mother at the end of the season since most of his pitiful earnings are needed to provide him with 2 meals a day. In the middle of all this beauty there is so much that needs addressing.

Godavari Botanical Gardens is about an hour's drive out of the city – all this way for seven rupees – not even 10p. The bus stops at a sheltered spot under the trees. I follow the road weaving downhill. Godavari village is a small cluster of houses on the left. To the right a stile over a wall indicates the back entry to the park presided over by an ancient man who asks for a 25 rupee entrance charge and no, has no change. I find a shop selling Sprite and return with change.

The park is a peaceful spot, with a stream flowing through the centre and different themed gardens. To the left, as you climb the hill, there is another steep section with greenhouses. Many of the plants are familiar – we have assimilated many Himalayan botanical species. To the right there are trails up under the trees that peter out at the boundary walls. The whole park can be walked round in 40 minutes but I am in no hurry. I have come for a peaceful day and it is very re-energising to sit in the fresh air in this green haven in the shadow of the Pulchowki mountain range. This is also clearly a place for courting couples. I have to avert my eyes discreetly, passing them locked in various passionate embraces, in shady sections of the park.

Surprisingly, there is one other European in the park, a tall, gaunt woman with grey hair. A young Nepali woman accompanies her. From the snatches of conversation that drift my way I realise she is American. She does not notice me, I seem to be good at blending into the background, and outside the tourist areas white women are an unexpected sight.

Back in Patan the shops are a lively as ever and I stop to check the prices of this and that and return with a couple of CDs. It's dark by 7pm and I am glad I have brought a torch to negotiate the dark lanes and avoid cars, cows and scavenging dogs sniffing through the rubbish. I know that the weather has changed because I am bitten by mosquitoes as soon as I get into bed, and realise that the time has come to use the insect plug, only to find I have no socket with the right adapter. I smear myself with Jungle Formula instead.

Monday March 11th
The woman in the park

When I cycle down to Pushapati for my 7 am start, I find the temple and the area surrounding it alive with coloured lights. There is much activity and a sense of anticipation in the air. Tents are going up on the land surrounding the temple in preparation for tomorrow's *Maha Shivaratri* festival, which celebrates Shiva's birthday with a great fair that pulls pilgrims from all over India as well as Nepal. The king will be attending the celebrations.

Today I draw a human shape on the blackboard and ask the children to name all the body parts. Then we sing *Head shoulders knees and toes*, *One finger one thumb keep moving*, and *Ten green bottles*, using my empty green Sprite bottle from yesterday as a prop. Someone has been down this road before as they know the words at least of the first two songs.

There is a representative from UCEP here today and I am introduced. No sign of Rajan. By the end of the session there are another 73 people in the world who can sing *Ten green bottles* – I am not sure how useful this is.

Back at the other school I feel at a loose end. Niam, the Vice-Principal asks if I'm lonely – Oh dear, what vibes am I sending out? I reassure him I am enjoying my privacy and the novelty of having a place to myself and discover I mean it. I appear to have twelve new e-mails until I discover nine are from my daughters Emma and Julia – Emma has sent the same one six times wishing me a Happy Mother's Day and one moaning about her flat mate.

I get a lift to Namaste supermarket, to collect up supplies and then find I have insufficient local currency when I get to the till. I negotiate to change some dollars but not before the American woman in the queue offers to help me out. It is the woman from Godavari Park and she is somewhat taken aback when I tell her I saw her there. We have a brief chat and it turns out she is here doing research for a project on child labour! Small world! I give her my e-mail, and we agree to meet and exchange notes.

I drag myself down to the Patan branch of Pilgrims bookshop to upgrade my English Nepali Dictionary to one with Nepali script, the better to suit Nima who is coming for an English class at 6pm. Nima arrives with two large-print, abridged copies of *The Adventures of Tom Sawyer* and *The Time Machine.* He haltingly reads the first four pages of Well's classic for me to assess his reading skills, punctuated with frequent loud nasal snorts. I doubt there is a soul in this city of diesel pollution free from nasal congestion. I set him a letter-writing project for Wednesday.

There is a gathering of males in the accounts office downstairs. Ashok introduces me to Nepali fast food, Mo mos – small dumplings that come with their own hot sauce, and they're delicious. I would happily swap the entire boxful for my Daal Bhat which arrives on cue, so I leave them to it.

Tuesday March 12th
Maha Shivaratri

I have got it into my head to create a small garden on the roof and having surreptitiously transferred some of the hundreds of flower pots from the entrance downstairs, I visit the local nursery and return with a palm, a small rhododendron and some daisies. The extra bit of greenery makes all the difference to the roof.

I have decided I should go to see the festival this evening, but when I telephone Ram he tells me the best part was early morning when the nearly naked saddhus cover themselves with ash from head to toe and contort their bodies into amazing yoga positions. Rani suggests Sabitha, Ashok's sister as a companion and she agrees to take me there on her motor bike. Ashok cautions us not to stay too long. 'There are people on drugs there,' he says.

The streets are nearly deserted till a mile from the temple and then they get so congested we decide to go the rest of the way on foot. Sabitha is lovely. She is 22 and the youngest in her family. Her job, motorbike and Western clothes mark her out from the older generation of Nepali women. As we walk towards the temple the crowds thicken. Two holy men out for alms try and anoint my forehead. Trying not to lose Sabitha in the crowd, I dodge the proffered mark. The saddhu glares at me in outrage. Oh dear, I think I have just lost some karma.

The police are out in force as the king's car is due any time. In the event, we see neither king nor temple. Near the Gausala roundabout, the crush between pilgrims moving in different directions becomes so intense I momentarily lose Sabitha in a sea of heads and for a few minutes am trapped in a solid wall of human flesh and cannot breath – terrifying.

We move to another vantage point, but then the crowd shrieks and begins to run back up the road. 'What's the problem?' I ask. 'They say there is a bomb' says Sabitha. 'Oh,' I reply, feigning nonchalance, 'shall we walk back up the road too then?' 'They've probably only said that to clear the road,' she says. 'Sure,' I say, but when we reach the next intersection and she suggests we might like to fight our way through another group of pilgrims in the gathering gloom to reach the temple, I decline. My inquisitive mood has passed.

We drive to Patan as night draws in, past endless pilgrims squatting by roadside fires. Hundreds of candles illuminate the ancient temples in the square. The roof garden of the Cafe de Temple offers a bird's eye view of the square, while I am updated on Shyam's businesses, sports club acquisition, new hotel and travel company. Overseas reservations are 75% down this year and many staff have been laid off. Our conversation is interrupted by the proprietor telling us that he is locking up two hours early, because there are 'a lot of mad, drugged people about.' He urges us to get going – not a place for women etc, etc. They lift the iron bar to let us out. The square is a bit of a washout, dark, quiet and nearly deserted. Wherever they are, the mad druggies are keeping a low profile.

Wednesday March 13th
Rita, Rajan and Renu

I enter the side-gate into the main school to the sound of rock music. A group of older kids are knocking out a number on a couple of electric guitars, keyboard and drums in the open space below me. They are rather good. Rani tells me one of the guitarist's father is a Hindu Guru. Before he turns up for Founder's Day, she thinks the son should learn some devotional music as a balance.

Rani asks me to help launch a story-telling competition but computer problems stall my rewrite of her over-long document with its endless list of rules and regulations. One of the 'rules' for the competition is that pupils should adopt the dress code of their school. Frankly I wouldn't care if they came in a tea towel if they could write. I'm not sure how the candidates will tackle the theme either; they are asked to write about 'how a mythical Nepalese character might respond to some of our contemporary social problems.' I'm more interested in how modern-day Nepalis cope with current social problems.

The American woman from the grocery store has e-mailed her phone number and I give her a ring. She says it is serendipity. Her boss was due to come to give a presentation to Shuvatara on Friday as part of the sensitisation programme. She is coming too and we can network. Her name is Rita.

Thursday March 14th

Rajan is back at the morning school. He has been ill. Sovhit and I get the children to make clocks out of paper plates; some have finished in 5 minutes, some are still struggling nearly an hour later. It illustrates one of the most difficult aspects of this teaching. Working with so many different levels of ability and understanding makes finding a common topic very hard. Many of the pupils need the kind of individual support the class is unable to provide. Sovhit tells me one boy cannot even write his name.

I tackle Rajan about splitting the class back into grades – he is showing an American visitor round this morning. I suggest Sovhit runs a very basic class for beginners and I take the ones who are a bit more advanced. He agrees. He is going to contact Rani about what help might be useful. I remind him I will not be staying past the April term because the ILO project will absorb much of my time. Rajan produces four pictures of his cousin's wedding and tells me I can keep them. I am delighted because it had seemed presumptuous to take a camera and now I have a record of the event.

Back at Shuvatara, despite a more sophisticated learning structure, there are still plenty of frustrations. Materials requested have once more not been supplied and the computer problems continue. Planning ahead is not part of the framework here. Trying to sort out the various problems, I arrive 20 minutes late for the ILO session.

The hall is packed. The main speaker is Dr Renu Rajbhandari, an incredible woman. She speaks mainly Nepali with the odd sentence thrown in, in English. The accompanying video is also in Nepali but she is so animated and passionate in her delivery I get the picture. She speaks to the children about child prostitution. She is a feminist doctor working for WOREC (Women's Rehabilitation Centre). We talk later. Her project is based near Pushapati, by the Gaurighat temple. I have arranged to visit her and hope to make a link for her with some British GPs.

The computer man cometh and eventually the problems are sorted. I am to get a small printer of my own to avoid incompatibility problems trying to transfer material from one computer to another. I am finally able to print out my revision of the story-telling rules for Rani. She likes the revised format, then – oh joy – she produces a package for me – a favourite CD I have been waiting to arrive from the UK. I had given up on the postal system.

Ram has e-mailed Rani, and she thinks they should buy his chalk. I have got several e-mails from trekkers promising to help, and suggesting they all donate £10 per month to the orphanage. In the event, the Internet is down so I cannot send replies. Rani has requested me to ask a visitor from England to bring out some AS papers and I cannot send this either. I leave a note asking the office secretary to please send the message first thing in the morning. This is crazy, I find myself thinking – a school with only two servers and one printer. Then I do a double take. The school I taught at this morning had no electricity.

I am half an hour late back to for my lesson with Nima to find he has been and gone. He phones at 9pm. I tell him how sorry I am that I missed him but he doesn't seem too put out. We arrange to meet tomorrow. Sarah, a textile specialist from the UK, has arrived in Nepal for five months. A bit of an old hand, she has agreed to come and help with the cats project next week. She says it is so easy to slip into all kinds of projects in Nepal. How right she is.

Friday March 15th

At morning school we look at the topic of food. I am aware that for many of the children eating regularly is one of the potential attractions of domestic service, though that will obviously vary, just as the overall treatment of domestics varies from employer to employer.

I read them *The Gingerbread Man* and *The Magic Porridge Pot* as examples of European folk tales about food and they brighten considerably, (we all have porridge in our respective diets). I think they are getting used to me because I had to get quite sharp with some kid picking a fight with another boy. They look shocked – they didn't know I can do fierce. Back at Shuvatara I find the school secretary has not sent the Principal's requested email. He suggests I do it in the computer room myself despite the fact that I am doing this as a favour for the school.

I'm on time to meet the Human Rights speaker Gopal Siwakoti, and my new acquaintance Rita. I can't follow a lot of the talk because it is in Nepali since 20 of the CWIN (Child Workers in Nepal) children are there, but the main point that seems to be coming across is, that what we are dealing with needs to be treated as a serious crime and not merely a 'social problem.' Gopal makes the point that trafficking is systematic, well-organised and makes quick and extremely high profits for the traffickers. It's exploitative, involves coercion, and the victim has no choice in the matter. He highlights a poem written by a secondary school pupil to the Kathmandu Post, about the guilt she felt realising that a child she saw regularly in the neighbourhood, who was clearly 'at risk', had 'disappeared.' He urges the audience not to pass by on the other side but tells them that the problem is happening under their noses. Vigilance from everyone, both young and old, is needed. The message is 'intervene.'

'Well,' says Rita to Gopal when the talk is over, 'no-one tried to stab you' – he looks quizzical. 'It's the Ides of March – March 15th,' she says. We go for some refreshments and I receive my second CD package in two days, Miles Davis' *Kind of Blue*. Rita says there is a Jazz Festival next week and perhaps we can go together. Sarah calls and invites me to an Art exhibition on Sunday at a prestigious gallery in a major complex called Barbar Mahal Revisited.

Saturday March 16th
Pushipatinath and an Invite to lunch

Nima arrives for more tuition prompt at 9am and I help him with a business letter. He wants to set up his own trekking business. Rajan and Amrit have invited me to lunch.

I cycle to Pushapati and, arriving early, decide to visit the grounds of the Temple. I am directed to a booth for a ticket and then a 'guide' attaches himself telling me things about the site I have already read. I just cannot shake him off. We go over a bridge and there to the right are the funeral ghats. Two bodies are burning, though there is no longer any recognisable shape – the process takes three hours apparently. As I watch, a third body wrapped in a blue sheet and garlanded in orange flowers is carried out onto another ghat.

I walk along the opposite bank and notice, with some distaste, that a group of tourists are aiming telescopic cameras at the ceremony. I feel angry at their insensitivity. 'You can take photos,' says my persistent guide. I tell him I do not want to – that this ceremony is for the loved ones, not for us. I explain that in England people would be angry if photos were taken of people in mourning, which is why I am ashamed of the lack of respect being shown by the tourists.

Nonetheless I cannot stop myself watching in fascination as sheaves of straw are piled up around and over the body. I am suddenly overcome by grief. The wasted body I have seen them lift effortlessly on to the pile of wood reminds me so much of my father when he died of TB, even down to the blue winding sheet that I selected to cover his body – God, I do miss him.

I walk back out of the temple pursued by my 'guide' – 'We can be friends,' he pleads. Amrit rescues me in the nick of time and my guide melts away. Amrit and Rajan live twenty minutes' walk from the temple. Their small, one-storey home down an unmade road, is in the grounds of another family house. Amrit tells me they came to Kathmandu from Pokhara to go to University. Amrit read Economics at Tribuhivan, Rajan, Business Studies.

Rajan greets me with green streaks in his hair. I have obviously caught him in the process of applying a new layer of henna. I am made very welcome – shoes come off at the door and I sit on cushions in their small living room while Rajan finishes the cooking. A cousin arrives, who works in the tourist industry. He quizzes me about where I have been in the world and offers to arrange all kinds of trips, but cools to the idea when I tell him I prefer to travel on local buses.

They are sociable and pleasant – they serve me a Daal Bhat and a delicious dessert rice pudding – with slices of coconut and a lot of ground cardamom. Amrit asks if he can have a go on my bike and disappears with it. By 3pm I have exhausted Rajan's extensive collection of travel photographs – he is remarkably well-travelled – and I feel it is time to leave.

Sunday March 17th
Babar Mahal and Rita revisited

Rani is at the annexe early supervising an Arts and Craft class. She comes for tea on my balcony and admires the 'garden.' Rita arrives for lunch. She tells me she's a Mennonite from Virginia, once married to a guy from Sierra Leone; she has been alone for sometime. This journey is partly research for her Masters in Peace Studies and partly a 'finding yourself' exercise.

We arrange to meet later at the Bagmati Bridge to go to the exhibition. I do a diversion to the Summit Hotel, a modern, luxury complex situated up a steep hill, for details of the Wednesday Jazz Festival. On my way back down to the bridge the heavens open, accompanied by a dramatic electric storm. I duck into a small bookshop and buy a city map and a poetry anthology called *The Child of Stone,* which is to prove inspirational when compiling the play.

Just as I have given up on Rita, a tall, elegant gentleman asks me if I am waiting for a friend and is she American? He has come out with his umbrella to guide me to where Rita is taking shelter. We hail a cab.

Babar Mahal is set in the renovated stables and courtyards of a magnificent former Palace. Nepali arts and crafts are displayed here at their best. The woman who started the Siddhartha gallery in the complex looks about eighteen but says she has a daughter on the brink of leaving home. The complex has been restored by a conservation trust and is a fine example of what can be done when money is no object. The atmosphere is 100% western. Rajan who arrives with his cousin, looks uncomfortable and clearly makes little of the contemporary Japanese prints. Rita, on the other hand, emerges as a bit of a culture vulture, making all the obvious acquisitive noises (whatever she says to the contrary) of the collecting American.

Sarah is there and some of her friends – they seem part of a well-established group. Rita and I stay and eat at the restaurant and the food is quite delicious (wild mushroom quiche in walnut sauce, smoked aubergine with spaghetti and pine nuts and a strawberry pudding) The ginger and lemon drink is good too. I realise I am obsessing a bit on food – this is the first change from Dhal Bhat in weeks.

Rita asks about the Jazz Festival, but having suggested it in the first place she is now very lukewarm, says she thinks it a bit expensive and that she knows where we can hear quite good jazz free of charge on a Wednesday night, so I agree to accompany her there instead.

Somewhere in the course of the evening I think my ears are playing tricks on me – with my dodgy hearing this happens all the time. She has been discussing relationships and saying that as part of her life change she feels she should open up more to new possibilities. Then I think she says, 'I'd like to have sex with you.' I ignore the comment. I must have misheard. Better to assume she hasn't said it, rather than she has. Life is complicated enough. We pick our way back through the dark flooded street down to the main road to catch a cab.

Monday March 18th

When I get to the morning programme the classes had not been divided as I had hoped, which is just as well because Sovhit does not show up this morning. I struggle on with both classes. Work on rudimentary grammar continues to be an uphill struggle. I get little response, even to tell me they don't understand. However *The Three Billy Goats Gruff* which I read to them as light relief, goes down well!

Classes end early this week because the host school has exams. All the schools have brought forward the dates of the exams because of the imminent Bhund called by the Maoists – the third since I got here. A Bhund is defined as 'the severest form of strike where all shops, schools and offices are closed and vehicles don't use the roads'. I have no way of measuring what they are achieving politically, if anything.

Stomach upsets are a necessary corollary of extended stays in Nepal. I feel too unwell to go into the school, a penalty of yesterday's rich food, except to hear the speaker from CWIN – Child Workers in Nepal – again all in Nepali. I am bothered that only six street children have turned up. Although they sit in the middle of the Shuvatara children, no one seems to make a move to socialise or talk to them. I arrange to visit CWIN's headquarters for extra research.

Tuesday March 19th
WOREC

Today I insist to a rather startled Amrit that the classes are put into separate rooms ***now***. Mission accomplished, I leave Sovhit to his own devices and set about reorganising my depleted group. We reconfigure the desks so that the kids can face each other – a totally novel idea for them, and play Alphabet Snap which introduces lots of new words. We play it twice because they are having such fun, and education and fun don't usually go together in Nepal, more's the pity.

I have managed to get an interview at nine this morning with Dr Renu. The Women's Rehabilitation Centre is a big, three-storey brick building but the sign is not very visible, and without Rajan's help I doubt I would have found it. Renu arranges a supply of material, including two videos and a tape of Nepalese anti-trafficking songs sung by the women of WOREC, for me to take away.

I discuss what medical help she would like from the UK, as I know medics who might be interested in assisting the project. She thinks their time would be more valuable than supplies. WOREC can find translators but not enough doctors. She says that one of the problems with this work is to avoid the backlash from the traditionalists who believe that trafficked women should be kept more vigilantly within the family, whereas girls who have escaped from the sex trade want to live a freer, independent life now. Before I leave I am shown all the knitwear the girls make in their skills centre and I order a cardigan for my step-daughter's new baby and one for myself.

I revisit Babar Mahal on my way back, to look at all the outlets I missed on the previous visit. A lot of shops are still empty. There is a traditional paper shop and one selling furniture, textiles, ceramics and other craft items. The quality and craftsmanship is marvellous. A rather upmarket clothes outlet is selling jumpers at a comparable price to those being sold by WOREC. I am glad to see they are aware of the commercial prices! I covet a black pashmina dressing gown at First World prices, well beyond my means.

I get back to Shuvatara feeling in need of a shower from the filth of the road. The pollution levels are truly awful, as awful as the road sense of Nepalis – pedestrians and drivers alike.

I am beginning to get very aggressive on the bike having had a few near misses with people who walk right out in front of me, or swing car doors open as I pass. Pedestrians show a clear preference for walking in the road even where pavements exist. This morning I saw a woman charge across the road without looking to left or right and end up almost under the wheels of a motorbike. Unlike back home, there is no moral righteousness about having 'right of way'. However suicidal or inconsiderate the pedestrian or driver, no one in Nepal passes judgements because there do not seem to be any rules anyway. A country that has to divert planes because there is a cow on the runway is unlikely to bother with a highway code.

I leave school about four with Rani. She points out the impressive building that will shortly house her husband's International Sports Club. The architecture is similar to the Babar Mahal. Built in a square with apartments to the rear, and a large central courtyard housing the shell of a swimming pool, there is a large, floodlit open-air dining area and bar as well as an internal bar and restaurant. I am told there will also be a very large function room upstairs, sauna, steam room, massage, and room for aerobics and yoga. Outside by the entrance there are tennis courts. As it is not in a tourist area, even when there are tourists, it suggests a large local elite. The contrasts in life-style here never cease to disconcert me.

Wednesday March 20th

I use picture cards at morning school in an attempt to get the children to make a story out of them. I have already removed ones which I think will be culturally meaningless, but even then they find the exercise very difficult. They have not been encouraged to use their imagination or to make choices.

But I am also part of the problem. Even when I think I have made enough cultural allowances I realise how little I understand their lives. A bunch of bananas, an apple and a kite might suggest a picnic and kite flying in a park to me – it is hardly a connection they are likely to make in a life devoid of leisure and toys.

I return to Shuvatara. Chandreyan wishes me to do a session on report-writing with the teaching staff. The session goes fairly well, although it is a little tricky explaining that phrases like 'she is a well-endowed girl' can mean something other than 'gifted.'

That evening when I ring Rita she announces she is going to the jazz concert I originally wanted to go to. She is unapologetic and off-hand. We were supposed to be going together, after all. I am annoyed and upset. I have coped with various minor inconveniences and mishaps at Shuvatara because, on balance, the school has made me feel useful and wanted. Now, this woman has made me realise how vulnerable I still am to any suggestion of rejection. I am disturbed at how much her dismissive rudeness is affecting me. Much later, with less than an hour before the concert ends, Rita phones back to offer me her ticket as she 'doesn't feel up to it.' She informs me she had already offered the ticket to someone in her house but he can't find his car keys! She then has the cheek to say she is still interested in coming to Pokahara with me. She must be joking. It confirms my long-held belief that if you want to do something, you are best off doing it alone.

Thursday March 21st
Art and artists

This is my second-to-last day on the morning programme. I have decided that since the children are celebrating Holi next week and have then finished their term, it is a natural time for me to leave.

I lunch with Rani and Sarah, who despite her preference to work in government schools, seems interested in making an input at Shuvatara. Rani can be very persuasive. Sarah has a textile commission to redesign the weave on the traditional Nepali red wedding veil, having previously worked on a similar Arts Council commission in Kuala Lumpur, Malaysia. She shows us interesting examples of her work.

We are introduced to Shoba, the new Shuvatara art teacher, and within minutes they have established a mutual link with Lorna, a UK art teacher who Sarah is staying with. Lorna, married to a Nepali, runs a Guest House and a trekking company in Kathmandu for six months of the year and lives in the UK for the other six months. I know her through the Nepalese Association in Manchester. Rani asks Sarah to introduce her to Lorna who has been a teacher of Art and Design for 30 years, because she thinks she can offer new ideas to her teachers.

Sarah comes back with me to look round the art room. She is shocked by the almost complete absence of work and thinks the new teacher can only make an improvement. We discuss Non-Government Agencies (NGOs) in Nepal. It seems many of the employees are paid First World wages, even though they are living in a poor country where their spending power is much greater than at home. To afford these foreign consultants, Nepal borrows at heavy interest repayment rates from the banks, which creates an even greater cycle of poverty. I suspect there are a lot of people out here in highly placed positions they would not warrant at home – she does not disagree. I am left with the impression that many of the NGOs are as inefficient as the Government Departments, which is alarming. I share my teaching problems on the morning programme. Sarah promises to come and give me a hand tomorrow.

Friday March 22nd

With Sarah at the morning programme the collage session we have planned goes well. The children are happy to learn in this way although they are uncertain of the names of colours like purple and pink and can't pronounce the 'y' in yellow. At one point Sarah illustrates what kind of thing they might make and immediately five little girls copy her exactly, illustrating my point that they have problems thinking independently.

Even so, by the end of the session those five collages have acquired slightly individual looks and it is tantalising and frustrating to think what these children might achieve with well-trained local teachers and proper resources. The next class also responds happily to this new kind of lesson, but again it takes a bit of time to pick up any creative ideas. I photograph them with their art work at the end of the session and their faces are a delight to behold.

Photo: © Hazel Roy

Rajan's cousin Bhakta collects me on his motorbike. He has brought me some literature on Pokhara and later he and Rajan accompany me to the Gongabu bus station to buy a ticket for my trip tomorrow. I am told I am 'lion hearted' going on a local bus. I don't know why. When we get back to New Baneshwar everyone is hungry. I suggest we get a bite to eat at the local Nanglos as I have a discount card. They eat heartily but will not let me pay. This makes me uneasy. I have already accepted their hospitality and am keen to make a return.

My unease increases when Bhakta offers me a lift back to the school on his motorbike. On the way, he tells me he wants to come to England but needs a sponsor. Remembering various warnings about the hazards of sponsorship I ask him what it involves. He breezily dismisses the question and does not answer me when I ask if one of the attractions is to work in the UK.

Saturday March 23rd.
A Trip to Pokhara – Nepal's Lake District

In the hubbub of early morning travellers, none of whom speak English, it proves difficult finding my bus. Eventually a small, rotund Buddhist priest dressed in saffron robes and a maroon woolly jumper shows me the right one and we climb in, over a large box apparently housing a television, plus huge trunks and cases that look as if they have been brought from the airport. The bus sets off three-quarters of an hour late – loaded to the gills – the open door offering the only air-conditioning.

The ancient vehicle, belching out black diesel fumes, climbs steeply with much changing of gears and creaks and groans. We rise out of the dust of Kathmandu and are soon in the hills overlooking dusty, orange, terraced fields, like corrugated cardboard, reaching away in serried ranks below us. The bus rounds the bend at the top of the mountain and we descend into richer green terraces and are soon passing by the luminous green of young rice fields in the valley. Labourers, bare footed and up to their ankles in mud, lead oxen yoked to primitive ploughs through the waterlogged fields.

I try and read one of the WOREC reports I have brought with me but cannot keep my eyes open and in no time I am drifting off to sleep, to be nudged awake by the plump little monk at my side. 'Repast,' he says. The bus has pulled in alongside a little tin shack and the passengers are soon making short work of tin trays of rice, vegetables and Daal Bhat. My stomach can't face it at 9am and since there are no other options, I fetch my sandwiches from the coach and order black tea.

Two hours of jolting through increasingly strong sunlight and an increasingly lush countryside full of kerbside palms and small rural thatched farms and there is a second longer break at a larger restaurant. I am amused to see my Buddhist companion hare up the stairs for a repeat Daal Bhat barely before the first one can have been digested. No wonder he is as round and smooth as a little brown nut.

I watch a languid young couple. She has henna tattoos all up her arm and silver jewellery on her fingers, her wrists and her ankles. I figure them as a honeymoon couple. There is something very constrained and detached about them.

The muse is broken by the bus horn. We do not stop again till we reach the outskirts of Pokhara. There is some delay at the first stop as the owner of the vast TV has difficulty forcing it down the aisle and half the passengers have to dismount so he can get it down the steps. His huge airport trunk is even more problematic and the conductor has to dismantle a seat to extract it! There are sighs of relief all round when it is finally all handed down into the care of a grim-faced, elderly matriarch with wrinkles like a walnut, who has come to ensure all the family purchases are safely removed from the bus.

I am ejected at the next bus stop – the last stop for Lakeside. I have already decided where I would like to stay, but have problems with a desperate rival agent who jumps into the taxi and tries to insist I look at his rather grim-looking hotel on the outskirts first. He is only deterred when I tell him I will get out of the cab if he doesn't. Although my destination is a popular hotel right by the lake, the cab has only worked out the route to Hotel Hong Kong and has to stop twice and reverse. Eventually with the aid of the map we get there.

I have picked Hotel Fewa, (an Americanism – the name of the lake is Phewa) deliberately for its idyllic location. I negotiate a room for $13 dollars a night, which is less than the rate quoted in a two-year old guide book written prior to the State of Emergency. I am given a pleasant room overlooking a garden and the lake, with an attractive balcony and reading area. I pounce on *100 Years of Solitude,* an appropriate holiday read, it's years since I read it .

The hotel food is largely American-Mexican, and with steak on the menu is clearly catering for tourists. It is so hot I pay one of the boatmen to row me out into the middle of the lake for a swim. The water is delightfully warm, with a view of the mountains thrown in. The best views are very early in the morning, when it is possible to see the Annapurnas in the distance but I can at least see up the hill to Sarangkot and the World Peace Pagoda, a Buddhist stupa which glints white and gold in the sun and forms a classic landmark on the skyline of Pokhara. Getting back in the boat is a bit of a struggle. The boat man has to give me a hand. I suddenly have a thought. 'Are there water snakes in the lake?' I ask. 'Oh yes, Miss,' beams my rescuer. I feel a bit faint. Just as well I have only discovered that now. Later I find there were other hazards from swimming in Lake Phewa I had not fully appreciated. A case of fools jumping in – literally!

In the evening I stroll around the town feeling like a tourist for the first time, but a tourist in a ghost town nonetheless. I even buy a lightweight Gortex jacket. I hadn't intended to, but the shopkeeper points out it is a bargain and it is indeed, nearly nine times cheaper than similar jackets in England. So who soaks up the difference? Not the poor sods making or selling them out here, that's for sure. The shop keeper tells me business has been terrible all year.

With this in mind, I am saddened to keep turning down the endless demands to step inside other shops and the Tibetan ladies with rucksacks full of jewellery that I do not want. There is an underlying sense of desperation in the exchanges which drives me back to the hotel early, but, with just a handful of tourists, the candle-lit, open-air restaurant seems bleak and unwelcoming.

Sunday March 24th – Tuesday March 26th

Wishing to escape the town and its sense of quiet despair, I take an early Sunday morning boat ride across the lake and hike to the peace pagoda on the opposite hill, a deceptively rigorous walk. Near the shore the boatman shows me an American holiday home, an old, traditional thatched farmhouse with a stone outbuilding which is occupied only two months of the year, and for which he acts as caretaker. It seems sad it is shut up for so long when it could supply a good home for someone local.

The stupa has all the magnificence of a film-set, in stark contrast to the simplicity of the farms I see as I start to descend on the opposite side of the mountain. I hear, rather than see a bellowing bull locked in a barn, and on the verandah of a small house what is, at first glance, a small straw cradle swinging under it own propulsion till I spot an ageing grandma stretched out on a straw mat pulling a string rhythmically to rock the baby.

On this side of the mountain the scenery is bleaker and harsher. On my way down I am surrounded by giggling young women in saris with docas on their backs. They have seen me stop to put suntan cream on my arms and stretch out their arms, insisting they have a spray too. Further down the hill I meet them again as a young man helps them fill their baskets with large boulders. One woman is dropping rocks over her shoulders into the basket, held in place by the thick band on her forehead. It is tough work for women. The contrast to their frivolity a few minutes earlier is unsettling.

The outskirts of Pokhara are dull to a degree. There is some nasty ribbon development and ugly, modern, cement houses for several miles before I reach Pokhara airport. I get my bearings back to the Lakeside, where I enjoy a fantastic meal of fish in ginger, served on a sizzling iron griddle. I am the only customer.

The following day I go for another row on the lake. In this land-locked country it is good to be near water. Much as I have enjoyed the tranquillity I am hankering to get back. I book a ticket back on the tourist bus for the following day, which for some reason is cheaper than the local bus, and spend the last night in the company of Mike from Kenya who has sold his market garden and is touring the world.

I shall remember Pokhara best for the early dawn sunrise over the lake and the serenity of its setting, but it is impossible to ignore the sense of despondency created by the recession in the tourist trade.

The return trip on the tourist bus has none of the character or atmosphere of the local bus ride, no Buddhist monks, no furniture removal, just a few lorries overtaking on hairpin bends on the wrong side. The bus is full of bulky, middle-aged German males dressed in shorts. I am aware that uncovered women's legs are considered unseemly in Nepal – a pity this convention does not extend to men.

Kathmandu looks so dusty and poor as we enter the outskirts of the city. I am hoping there will be a lot to keep me busy to justify an early return.

Wednesday March 27th

No one is around. I finally get through to the ILO by phone to be told Sunil Pokharel, the Artistic Director of Aarohan Theatre, has been appointed to work with me on the drama project. After several attempts, I get Sunil on his mobile and invite him for breakfast on Friday.

I share some of my reservations about the sensitisation programme with Bimal and he agrees with me; the kids are losing the feel for the project, the result of sitting in an overheated hall and being lectured at. We need to get a more interactive approach going soon.

I cycle to the supermarket for supplies, aware the shops may be closed during Holi. It is pitch black when I leave. I have asked for yoghurt, not expecting it to come in a large earthenware pot. With a weighty haversack on my bag already, it leads me to wonder if I can pick it up tomorrow, but when I ask if they are open on Holi, repeatedly the answer is 'Maybe.' No, they are not making fun of me, they just don't want to disappoint me. Eventually they admit the shop will be shut. I cycle back precariously.

Thursday March 28th
Holi Holi Holi

'This exciting festival is closely related to the water festivals of Thailand and Myanmar and takes place on the full-moon day in the month of Falgun (February to March). By this time, late in the dry season, it is beginning to get rather hot and the water, which is sprayed around so liberally in the festival is a reminder of the cooling monsoon days to come. Holi is also known as the Festival of Colours and as well as spraying water on everything and everyone, coloured powder (particularly red) and coloured water are also dispensed. Foreigners get special attention.'
Lonely Planet Nepal Guide 2001

I wake early full of nervous energy, feeling cooped up. By 9am I have cleaned everything in the place and I am beginning to feel under house arrest. The day is warming up and I want to be out and about. Given the heat of the day, being sprayed with water doesn't sound that bad. I fish out my oldest clothes, so if I do get spattered with red or coloured powder it won't matter too much and decide to take a chance.

I have worked out a route to the Nagarjun Forest Reserve on the North West of the city, a mix of lanes and part way on the ring road which will take me past the Buddhist temple of Swayambhunath up on a hill to the west of Kathmandu, known as the monkey temple because of the large tribe of monkeys that swarm all over the site and feast regally on all the temple offerings – a chance to take in two places that I want to see.

Swayambhunath:Photo: © Hazel Roy

The route down to the Sanepa bridge is accompanied by no more than a few thin sprays of water squirted by kids with water pistols and I think if it is no more than that, I can cope with it. The problem starts after I cross the second bridge on the ring road and turn right on a road parallel with Durbar Square. As the lanes narrow I realise I may have taken on more than I bargained for. I am about to discover the extent of my naivety.

Holi, depending on your perspective, is either terrific fun or a mischievously aggressive festival. Children and youths into their early twenties roam the streets with plastic bags full of water which they hurl, like bombs, at passers-by. Foreigners are a particular target and foreign women on bikes, a rare sight at the best of times, are like manna from heaven. It's like every football crowd you have ever wanted to avoid combined with the inmates of the local lunatic asylum, all deciding that you are a particularly tasty target for their dangerous pranks.

The full realisation that I am target number one hits me with the first lot of water – we are not talking now about small water bombs but whole bucket loads thrown down with some force from five storeys above. I avoid the first two or three, but after that they get me full on target, and not just one bucket load will satisfy. I am drenched to the skin as bucket load follows bucket load all down the road. It is as if they had been waiting for a really fine target to aim at. One hits my back with a heavy thud that nearly knocks me off my bike – it is the bag variety of bomb but a very large one and thrown with considerable force. I am glad I am wearing a haversack to absorb some of the impact. I have no other option but to keep pedalling like hell while the baying laughter from youths covered from head to toe in red powder follows me down the narrow lanes and warns those ahead of the treat in store.

Of course there is plenty of water being sprayed around at other people but there is no doubt I am a particular target. It seems the festival gives gangs of youths the license to release all their normally well-repressed resentment against foreigners as well as a chance to react to the audacity of a woman committing the 'unnatural' act of cycling through the city. Bearing in mind that without the distraction of the water, these lanes are normally hazardous as you constantly have to swerve to avoid pedestrians, cars, motorbikes, cows and huge holes in the road, this added obstacle comes close to attempted murder as they frequently force me into the path of oncoming vehicles.

Despite being very careful to keep my legs and arms well covered when

I cycle, I have been coping for weeks with the astounded stares of Nepali males who see my presence on the road as a challenge to their manhood. Even on clapped-out bikes and loaded down with all manner of goods and chattels that cannot compete with my lightweight mountain bike, they have to try and overtake me. Now I am paying for my audacity in breaking their gender norms, for there are no young women hurling water that I can see. This is a sport for the lads.

My pumps squelching with every turn of the pedals I finally break loose from them on the long steep hill up to Swayambhunath. I am glad it is up a hill for by the time I spot the dome in the distance I have become so disorientated being constant target practice, I am unsure if I am going in the right direction – the simple directions I have written on a piece of paper in my pocket have been reduced to an indecipherable pâpier maché lump. The shrine, even after weeks of seeing numerous stupas is very impressive. Sadly I am not in the right frame of mind to appreciate it as much as I would have liked. I am trembling by the time I dismount, partly from nerves but also from what seems a naked and deep-seated display of aggression I have never experienced till now in Nepal. I climb the steps to the main monument tight-lipped – deaf to the constant clamour of the rupee beggars. The steps turn at right angles and ahead is the main stupa, a huge structure topped by a gold-coloured square block.

A solitary male figure far up on the top of the shrine is fixing new prayer flags over a huge dome which looks as if a giant cauldron of vivid saffron yellow has been poured over the white stonework. Below, the watchful eyes of the Buddha gaze out across Kathmandu valley. A third eye above the others indicates the Buddha's clairvoyant powers – clearly not something I was graced with today. The 'nose' that looks like a question mark is actually the Nepali number eke (one) a symbol of unity. Set around the base are a set of prayer wheels which can be spun as you pass and which contain the sacred mantra 'om mani padme hum' (repeated endlessly on a thousand CDs throughout the tourist quarter).

Today many candles are burning and butter candles are on sale for 5 rupees or more, to light at one of the shrines behind the stupa. There are small shrines with lighted candles and food offerings around the base and I am fascinated watching the monkeys delicately picking their way round the burning wax to get at the food.

I relax as well as someone can who is soaked to the skin and sit myself in the strongest sunlight in the rather lame hope of drying out. I notice a party of tourists covered with red powder who seem to have at least escaped the water. Suffering from an uncomfortably damp bum I get up and wander in and out of the centuries-old buildings that surround the stupa, alive with stalls selling brass knick-knacks, masks of the gods, and puppets.

Time to steel myself for the streets ahead, I return to collect my bike. At the base of the very steep hill I turn up and take the right hand road as indicated by a policeman. I am in an area called Balaju, near the public bus park and close to a large industrial estate. It is a poor area and there seems to be a direct relationship between the poverty of a suburb and the degree of ferocity with which the water is thrown. I sense trouble ahead and park up the bike to buy a Sprite from an elderly lady in a tiny shop with a young woman and little child sitting outside on stools. I feel partly protected in their presence and need to take stock of my directions.

A van squeals to a halt next to me. In the back are five or six young men with an array of orange buckets tied to ropes. They look at me meaningfully. I glare back as assertively as I can, making sure I am standing as close to the elderly shopkeeper as possible. Two of them get down and go to replenish the buckets with water. The van waits. I sense they are waiting for me to move off as well. A stationary target is not half as much fun as a moving one but where I am standing I don't think they would dare to chuck so much water. The young woman gets up and tucking her child on her hip moves off across the road. I want to shout out 'don't go please' but I clamp my teeth together and sit tight.

I look over the road to see the same young woman raising a huge sack of rice onto her back, positioned by a harness round her forehead. Behind her a man carries the much lighter child. Bloody men, I think. One of the men from the van carries out a box of San Miguel's from the back of the shop and tucks them behind the passenger seat. Another brings bags of crisps. I wait. Finally they are off. I turn round and cycle back down the road in the opposite direction no longer caring that it is carrying me off my route. The lane narrows and I get that sinking feeling again as I see the road ahead of me awash with water. By now my tolerance has disappeared. Bombarded with water again over my partially dry clothes I select a few choice epithets for the bombers lining the rooftops with their buckets. They seem to enjoy my colourful colloquial English – indeed it seems to inspire them to greater efforts.

Just when I think I can endure it no longer the turnstiles of the Mahendra Park appear on my right and a guard opens the gates to let me park up the bike. On my map the nature reserve is to the rear of the park and it looks as if you can walk through from one to the other. I ask if this is the case and I am told it is, so I pay 5 rupees for admission. In the centre of the park I find a small cafe with some elderly Nepalis, bone dry and in their weekend best, sitting under a sun umbrella. I go and order some Mo mos and tea from the counter and drape my damp body on a bench near the family group.

Various roving gangs of lads wander into the park covered in red powder. I hold my breath but they pass on. Two young courting couples flirt at the table next to me. Obviously once young men gravitate to an interest in sex, the water bombs have less pulling power. None of them have a trace of red powder on them. I stroll cautiously in the park, trying to get dry, walking briskly past the 22 waterspouts, which are one of the park's main features, under which various young men are washing themselves vigorously.

Past a couple of small temples I follow a 'picnic trail' up into the trees at the rear of the park that looks as if it might give on to the nature reserve, but without success. As in Govinda, the park is well walled with barbed wire reinforcements. I retrace my steps and stop to ask two women near the park gates whether a lane to their right leads up to the reserve. They do not understand me. Next thing I know I am surrounded by young men asking me where I want to go, where I am from and what do I think of Nepal. It is a bad day to ask me such questions. They offer to escort me to the reserve, back along the route I have previously come, but suddenly I have had enough. No, I say. I am sick of Holi, I want to go home. The park attendant assures me that if I follow the road to the right I will hit the Ring Road and I manage to get down there without getting significantly wetter.

Normally I would avoid the Ring Road like the plague, not only because it is a long way round but also because the pollution levels from the traffic belching out black diesel fumes are appalling, but today lead poisoning seems the lesser of the two evils. I figure that with the buildings further back from the road I can make the bulk of the journey hazard free. I get the odd water bomb but mostly my theory is borne out, until halfway back a small boy dashes out in the road ahead of me his hand raised above his head. He is running directly towards a bus and aiming for me. He causes me to swerve almost into the bus as the missile hits me hard on the neck. I swear – colourfully.

I proceed, shaken by my closest encounter yet with death in South East Asia. Eventually I cross the river and see the sign for Sanepa that shortly brings me up a narrow lane by the side of Rani's house. In 10 minutes I am home, stripping off my damp clothes and under a hot shower.

Half an hour later, my washed clothes hanging on the line – my underwear stained blue from the water bombs – I am sitting on the roof terrace with a large G&T. The lads from the rooftop opposite, who have never made any attempt to talk to me before, call something out. I do not respond except to measure the distance between our roofs and wonder if I am safe to be out here in clean clothes.

I have been invited to an Art exhibition at 4pm at the Annapurna Hotel by Durbar Marg. It seems a suitably sedate end to a crazy day so I walk cautiously down to the taxi rank to see the only taxi pulling away. There is a filthy old auto rickshaw on the side of the road and I decide to give it a go. It is the slowest and most uncomfortable journey I have ever made (apart from the one I have just survived) and I lurch from side to side, with my stomach churning in protest.

We get to the Annapurna for the bargain price of 56 rupees but by now it feels as if someone has been shredding my inside. I find the exhibition in the back of this plush international hotel. It's pretty uninspiring and I have just been recognised by the artist, the art therapist who I met at Barbar Mahal Revisited, when I have to make excuses and dash for the loo.

When I return I ask her how she managed to end up with her leg in plaster. She is sitting in a wheelchair. Apparently, she fell and retracted her shoulder as well as breaking her leg. I ask what she is taking for the pain – is it Ipobrufen? 'Oh no,' she says, that would disagree with her IBS and her asthma. She looks the picture of health but she has survived three strokes in one year, which is why she is staying at a hotel – The Verge Inn – no, really. 'They look after me so well,' she murmurs, staring up at the young man pushing her chair.

I spot a familiar back. Rita is touring the exhibition with another woman. She is off-hand. I manage to get a cab home and then, suddenly, I feel very, very vulnerable and lonely. I go and lie on the bed in the darkening room and try to fight off the black mood listening to Miles Davis, which only makes me feel worse. Rita phones and suggests we do something together on Saturday. It is my fervent wish to agree and then stand her up. I give myself a talking-to for wallowing in self-pity. Holi was an experience, and experience usually comes at a price.

Friday March 29th
Sunil

Physically I am pretty below par for the breakfast meeting with my co-drama worker. Sunil is strikingly good-looking and could pass for 25. He certainly looks too young to have been involved with Aarohan Theatre for 20 years. I make tea and we sit out on the roof while I skim through a leaflet about the company's work.

Aarohan was established in 1982 by Sunil and four other actors. They describe their work as '*celebrating traditional Nepalese cultural diversity,*' particularly '*voices suppressed and forms of life rendered marginal by consumer culture and materialism*'. Their repertoire includes classics from the rest of the world (Sophocles, Brecht, Sartre, Camus) and supporting work by Indian playwrights.

In addition to Drama Festivals and theatre workshops, the company perform issue-based theatre in rural Nepal, on topics like women's rights, AIDS, community development, leprosy, health and education. They work with deaf people and street children and Save the Children US. UNICEF and many other agencies have supported them. They have broadcast a number of TV films and serials for Nepal TV. Future plans include establishing a performing arts school and undertaking the documentation of the Newari culture, much of which is on the verge of extinction.

Sunil trained as an actor in New Delhi and has been experimenting with Augusto Boal's Forum theatre techniques. I am delighted to be working with someone so experienced and on such a similar wavelength. I quickly bring him up to speed on my background.

The ILO session is chaotic – Sunil and I have devised some integration exercises but the CWIN lads don't show. There is a fairly predictable technical glitch and the video does not work. Instead Bimal rushes through some notes and hands over to me. I ask for those who want to be involved in the production to come and sign up.

Some of the children do not want to participate and who are we to force them? Chandreyan, the Vice-Principal is not happy about this and demands to know why they don't want to be involved. We manage to persuade him to let them leave without explanation. But then he has his own ideas about how the lists of participants are to be organised. He intervenes again when I introduce Sunil and again when we organise the drama games. The constant interference is counter-productive and embarrassing. I hope we will be left alone to run the project in future.

Fourteen students express interest in coming to the WOREC Open Day and I arrange to meet them at the Gausala roundabout at 11.30am on Monday. Sunil and I arrange various planning meetings for those interested in the production after the Bhund, which starts on Tuesday. We learn that ten young people from CWIN are to be involved. At last things are starting to happen.

Rita calls and tells me that a bucket bomb went off at the bridge by the CWIN office this morning injuring 31 people. She has picked it up on the Internet. There is no report on the news. I ring Sarah to see if she has heard about this and the rumour that the Maoists are going to target tourists soon. Sarah says there is a lot of scaremongering about. Apparently the head of the Maoists has issued a statement saying he is not targeting tourists. It is difficult to know what to believe. I get the impression Sarah is not robust in her approach to life, but then again she works with some politically astute people. I guess only time will tell.

Sunil invites me to see a version of Oedipus on Sunday at his old college and offers to introduce me to some theatre people in Kathmandu.

Saturday March 30th

Today I pick up a book in Pilgrims by the feminist sociologist Anne Oakley. Pilgrims is such an intriguing bookshop – you just never know what will turn up there. The book proves compulsive reading as I share many common experiences and mutual friends with the author, one of whom died quite tragically at the age of 25. I read her books with a sense of returning to the familiar. The world of radical feminism in 1970's Britain seems light years away from the experiences of most women in Nepal thirty years later. As I put the book down, the neighbourhood dogs set up a barking match which rises to frenzy level putting paid to any thought of sleep.

Sunday March 31st
Oedipus and a 'grand do'

A handwritten message arrives from Rani, inviting me to a 'grand do' at the Hyatt Hotel tonight, called 'Celebrating Womanhood.' I have a premonition of what it will be like. Formal dress is required, which in my case will have to be loosely interpreted.

I am also invited to the school's sports day which begins at 9.30am. I stagger downstairs because I can smell the kettle burning and almost into the arms of Sarah who is doing a morning session with Shoba. I make her tea, and then shower in cold water. The guards have an uncanny knack of turning off the hot water just when I want a shower. They are also good at locking me in when I want to get out, or locking me out when I want to get in.

Sports day is a big event with all kinds of unusual and elaborate races in the back sports field, serried ranks of elegantly dressed parents in the audience, a rostrum for the winners and lots of photographers. A school for disabled children has also attended and competed. I am told I have just missed the Minister.

Chandreyan is in his element urging on the children and announcing the winners in a huge proud voice, especially when one of them is his own chubby little daughter. 'She wraps him round her little finger already,' someone comments dryly. In the front playground catering stalls dispense hot snacks, coke, and ice cream for the visitors.

I leave to meet Sunil at Dili Bazar. The production of *Oedipus* is taking place in the basement of a cramped little theatre and is being produced by a 2nd year BA English group from a local college. I am introduced to a portly, elderly gentleman who is the Director.

The set consists of a black paper backdrop on which a door has been roughly outlined in chalk. On the walls are four masks – I know masks were an integral part of Greek theatre – but of Minnie Mouse? The production is scheduled to start at 2pm. In true Nepali style nothing happens till 2.45 though there is much peeking through the curtains. Students in neat little Greek tunics keep popping into the audience to socialise with friends. Eventually things get going, but the dialogue is drowned by a cacophonous sound-effect of barking dogs and lowing cows, presumably as rural scene-setting. The amplifier whistles and screeches in sympathy.

Oedipus in a long black satin tunic, clutching the hilt of his sword, drags himself onto the stage as if he has a wooden leg. Maybe he has, because he maintains this walks throughout the performance together with a stricken expression, which it becomes increasingly difficult to take seriously. The actors deliver their lines in parodic sing-song accents. The three soothsayers seem to have learned their routine from Monty Python. Meanwhile, the person on the dimmer switch (in the absence of theatrical lighting) takes the house lights up and down alternately throughout the performance, presumably in the belief that this adds to the dramatic effect. I doze off. I am nudged awake by Sunil to inform me he is slipping outside. Much as I would like to join him, I brave it out to the end.

The audience breaks into nervous laughter as one of the cast, who might have the glimmerings of an acting talent, announces the queen's death. This in turn affects those on stage, who can barely keep a straight face and by the time poor old Oedipus crawls on with red greasepaint smeared under each eye, the laughter is no longer muffled. It ends as all things must. I wait for the line-up and bow, but they are all introduced individually – it takes an age.

When it is over the elderly director turns to me and I pre-empt the question I am dreading by asking how long they rehearsed this for. 'Two weeks,' he says proudly. I am tempted to say 'that long?' but resist the desire. Sunil is outside smoking a cigarette. It has poured down while I have been incarcerated and my bike seat is drenched. 'What did you think of it?' I ask. 'It was awful,' he says. I am relieved. If he had said anything else I would regard the ILO project as doomed.

I cycle home through the rain, and call Rani to tell her I am back. Despite my best efforts I fail to look either formal or glamorous. The Kakshapatis are late. Rani is in a glittery sari. I am ushered into the back of a large sedan. Shyam is at the wheel, some ersatz pop on the radio. He does not acknowledge me. I am conscious as I chat to Rani on the long journey around the ring road in the dark – a rare occasion to be out after dark in Kathmandu – how attentive she is to Shyam, touching his arm, explaining something I said. I realise I am talking too fast because I am nervous. There is an atmosphere in the car.

The Hyatt is a long way out. It has a drive, which seems to go on for at least a mile, a vast floodlit approach with a huge fountain and a portico the size of an aircraft hangar. Rani tells me she loves the place. It is so grand they park the car for you. We wander into a vast marble lobby and down two grand staircases to an equally grand lower floor. I have been forewarned that we are attending a fashion show with a new twist - celebrating women of all ages and blending the traditional and the new in Nepali clothes designs. Free samples of a face cream called *'Fine and fair'* are being dispensed, which promises to reduce the melanin in your skin and give you a paler complexion.

We enter a massive conference room with a prosperous-looking audience of several hundred, who seem well acquainted. Rani informs me in whispers that this will be 'a very classy show' organised by their friend's daughter.

The evening is compeered by a man in a black glittery suit. He jokes that the audience might be wondering why he is introducing a show described *'In Celebration of Women'* and then, as if suddenly struck by the incongruity himself, he mutters something about having a mother, gets down from the rostrum and disappears.

A perky young woman in a similar black glittery outfit takes his place and introduces four models 'inspired by the elements'. This consists variously, of a model in a black two-piece, with a white moon halter neck and stars on her pantaloons, a model in flame-red silk, a model floating around with a white veil, surrounded by copious quantities of dry ice, and the last, presumably representing water, with two large blue fishes attached vertically down over her boobs and something that looks like a clump of green weed attached to the small of her back.

The models follow thick and fast, in ever more exotic creations. It's all quite surreal. Then to remind us the event is to celebrate women of all ages, an elegant young woman in black appears clutching the arm of a chubby toddler wearing a baseball cap, with a huge pink dummy clamped in his mouth. Holding his other arm is a glamorous grandmother sporting a red sari and a dazzling white smile. They stroll down the cat walk, the stumbling tot between them, flashing whiter than white smiles to tumultuous applause.

This is followed by a number celebrating *'The Hills of the Glorious Himalayas.'* I have an instant recall of a video I have been watching of newly 'empowered' hill women, swarthy, prematurely wrinkled, with nose rings and multi-coloured layers of clothes and head turbans. I cannot quite square this image with the six young sylphs in an array of white gowns 'inspired by the mountains'.

We are then treated to some rather risqúe adaptations on the traditional Hindu wedding outfit. The lady next to Rani mutters that no daughter of hers could expect to be wed in such a frivolous get-up. Rani decides this is a reasonable cue to exit for the buffet before the rush starts. The men are already outside, many like Shyam, with mobile phones to their ears. The bar is doing a roaring trade in whisky, which seems to be served exclusively to the men There is red wine for the women, but it is sour and unpalatable, and a lavish hotel buffet with lots of cream cakes. A woman is introduced who has a 14-year-old daughter at Shuvatara. She looks right through me and buttonholes Rani to invite her to a supper party. I reflect again on how invisible single women are out here.

We leave early and drive back in silence. We are stopped no less than eight times by very nervous-looking army patrols. The Kakshapatis confirm that the bridge bombing was on the news, but a day late. Tomorrow is the eve of another Maoist Bundh which will disrupt school examinations.

I appreciate why Rani wanted to leave early. On top of her domestic anxieties she has all the stresses and strains of living in a country on the brink of civil war where schools like hers are constantly targeted, yet where she strives so hard for improvements. I am feeling pretty strained too, so I am grateful when, back at the school, Shyam gets out of the car with me, rattles the locked gates and says something curt to the guard who takes his time coming out to unlock them.

The Project Takes Shape

Child workers in Nepal (CWIN), The price of bricks,
Nepalese new year, Pessimism and picnics,
In limbo in Chitwan, Our rehearsal space vanishes,
Dress rehearsal and D-Day

Monday April 1st

The printer has still not arrived, which is not surprising really when I find it has yet to be ordered. There is a picture and article announcing the death of the Queen Mother in a Nepalese paper.

I cycle to Guasala to meet the students to find only 3 have turned up. They are Probalta and younger sister Prashamsha, who speaks English with a curious transatlantic drawl. Both girls have spent time in the States. They are accompanied by Pukar, a tall, handsome lad, who is doing AS levels with Prashamsha. They are all very quiet and thoughtful with impeccable manners. I remember the route to WOREC and arrive in time for the performance at 12, only to find it has been cancelled.

We look round the exhibition instead. I introduce Pukar and the girls to the WOREC drama co-ordinator who speaks no English, and meet Renu's sixteen year old son Tskisi, who is running a youth project. The craft lady has the woolies ready that I ordered and relieves me of most of the money I had put aside for the week, and then says something about me being wealthy. I wait for Sunil, who was also coming to the performance. Eventually I phone him. He says he came at 12.30, was told that we had not arrived and had gone home again. He comes down to meet me at the Gausala roundabout on his motorbike and I follow him back to his house.

Sunil lives in any airy, ground floor apartment down a small unmade road. His wife has gone out to get provisions for several days because of the Bhund. A small delivery boy helps her carry back the parcels. There is nowhere free of child labour in this city. She says the prices have gone up because the traders have been capitalising on the fact that there will be nothing open for several days now.

Sunil and I settle down to discuss the SCREAM project. We agree the subject is so huge that the only way to tackle it as a piece of theatre is to focus on four children's stories – possibly looking at the trafficking of girls, rag pickers, children working in the brick industry and children in domestic service.

I agree to contact a number of the NGOs working in this field, for assistance setting up interviews for the children. Sunil has contacts he will also explore.

32 actors have signed up, plus a backstage cast, which gives us roughly eight actors for each 'story'. We talk about how we can foster commitment and involvement. We agree we must limit participation to those who show concern with the issues, as the CWIN children will quickly sense insincerity.

This might appear to be qualifying the aims of the project, but we have to be realistic about how little time we have and the ground that has to be covered. We cannot hope to win over all the children and have too little time to spare for those who are not really interested or cannot work to a strict timetable. That said, we have to inspire and energise and not be punitive or the enthusiasm and commitment will not happen. The project will still offer huge educational potential for all of us.

We discuss the time frame for interviews, the need to provide a guideline framework for questions and the work involved in feeding the material obtained back into the script. The deadlines are dauntingly tight. My experience to date suggests deadlines in Nepal are, at best, haphazardly understood. My only comfort is the fact that I am working with a professional theatre director who totally understands deadlines.

Before I leave, Sunil shows me a video he made in 1997 for Red Barna, the Danish 'Save the Children' organisation. The Film is called 'Life on the Street'. It is an exquisite 10-minute film without dialogue, following two young rag pickers through an average day on the streets of Kathmandu. It is so evocative and moving I want to find a way to use it in our production, because it encapsulates with economy and skill the lives of the street children. Sunil agrees to this suggestion.

Sunil's son brings home news that the Bhund is cancelled and that he is back in school tomorrow. The Maoists have given in to public pressure, as all the children's exams would have been affected by the strike.

Tuesday April 2nd

I wake early with the idea of writing lyrics for an opening song. The power supply has other ideas and cuts me off midstream. I handwrite the rest.

Chandreyan is in the main school and announces his intention of attending the first planning meeting for the production. I appreciate his need, as the permanent member of Shuvatara staff, to feel in some kind of overall charge, but I hope he will not cramp our style. I try to explain that we are confident to proceed alone, but he is not listening.

Terribly dramatic electric storm tonight – the first bang is so loud I drop to the floor wondering if it is a bomb. It is difficult to get some of the windows shut. Some of the plants on the roof garden are pounded to death. In the bathroom where there is only mesh at the windows the storms have driven thick black sooty earth into the bath again. The water seeps through the door to the flat roof and forms a pool outside my bedroom door.

Wednesday April 3rd
Time with Rani

I await the arrival of the second printer – the first proved incompatible. The printer men are quite early for a change and I leave them to it. I know it is considered respectful to remove shoes as you enter a room, but I would prefer to sweep up afterwards than live with the pungent smell of unwashed male feet. This is not an option I know they will consider, but reading my diary or shuffling randomly through my paperwork as they wait for the computer to warm up is fair game. I remove sheaves of paper away from curious eyes.

Sheila Bull from the Nepalese Association arrives on her twice-yearly trip to Nepal, with books she has kindly brought out for the school. I arrange for her to be reimbursed and show her around. She seems impressed by my self-sufficiency. We lunch with Rani, who is in fine form. She tells us she wants to go back to TV presentation work and then launches into a long monologue about educational reforms, punctuated by occasional questions fired mainly at Sheila, whom she is obviously sizing up.

Rani's background is an unusual one for a Nepali woman. The youngest of four, she was brought up rather unconventionally, though her parents were fairly traditional high-class Hindus. Rani's brother broke with tradition by marrying a Goanese woman and not moving her in to live with his parents, who lived in an isolated part of Darjeeling. Moreover, his wife was Catholic and he converted to Catholicism.

Despite being a Hindu, Rani was educated at a Catholic convent and again, uncharacteristically, all three daughters of the family have had careers. Rani's oldest sister Rita became a film and TV star, but when she became a widow she became a healer and a Buddhist. Her other sister went into business, opening a couple of restaurants, then moving to Malaysia where she married a Moslem who later converted to the Ba'hai faith.

Rani married a Newari man out of her caste. She says she still doesn't speak Newari but wishes she did, so she would know what her husband talks about to his grandmother's daughter (which seems a strange way to refer to Shyam's mother). Rani adds that while she rebelled against tradition when she was younger, she is coming round to a more traditional view.

Thursday April 4th

Rani invites me for lunch at a Japanese restaurant near Durbar Marg, to meet Sian, who is coming to Nepal for three years. Sian's husband is vice-Consul at the British Council. She is Head of Languages at a London secondary school and will be taking an MA in Japanese while she is here. Over lunch she tells us the British Council require their employees to live within the Ring Road and employ a security guard.

We discuss the current situation in Nepal. The Maoist leader apparently contacted the embassies some months ago to inform them that they were not targeting tourists, but would at the same time be stepping up their bombing campaign in the tourist areas. It is hardly reassuring for tourists to know that if they are killed it will be by accident rather than design. We discuss the educational situation and Rani is off, she has a messianic zeal about educational reform in Nepal.

After lunch, Rani insists I join her, reluctantly, at the hairdressers for a hair cut. I want to go to the photographers on New Road, so she has me driven there. New Road is a busy, scruffy, central thoroughfare where local people shop, and with a reputation for being the place you can get most things.

There is a slightly risky feel to the place. Beggars are very noticeable and persistent here. There is a tiny, dirty child sitting on the ground with an even tinier baby on his lap. They are filthy and look as if they have been there an age. He looks too tired to beg. I am very aware of these children, even more so since we started the ILO project. I wonder where his parents are, or if they are orphans. I still find it so hard being jolted between affluence and despair.

Freak Street is just round the corner, which is where the hippies all hung out in the 1960s. In its prime it was the place for cheap hotels, colourful restaurants, hashish shops and of course, the weird and wonderful 'freaks' who gave the street its name. Times change. The cheap hotels are still there but most independent tourists head now for Thamel. Shyam was brought up in Freak street and still has an ancient granny residing here.

I deposit camera film for development, Rani buys samosas and sweetmeats. We hunt down her chauffeur, not easy as the centre is packed. The road ahead leading to Durbar Square is uneasily thick with soldiers. Rani points out the Government newspaper office where she used to work as a journalist, and an ancient pipal tree, the focal point of the area and of great religious significance.

Friday April 5th
CWIN

I cycle to the CWIN offices, getting lost down winding lanes in a part of the city I am unfamiliar with. This makes me late for Gauri, who is otherwise engaged when I arrive. Instead, I talk to the charming Sushila, daughter of the AML leader who is familiar with Sunil and his work.

Gauri joins us with Shanta the project co-ordinator, and we discuss whether we should consider the brick industry within our story. Gauri thinks that with the carpet industry under scrutiny (the Rugmark symbol now indicates when a product has been produced free of child labour), there has been a drift of children away from the carpet industry into the even more hazardous brick industry. After the meeting Sushila shows me the library and I research material on the brick industry. I am moved by a story about one family in particular and how they came to be working on the brick site. It is a story I would like us to tell.

In the afternoon Rani and I visit Sarah and Lorna for afternoon tea. They live in a large, traditionally furnished house rented from a Ghurkha landlord. Lorna has designed the garden and keeps chickens. Buddhist prayer flags flutter in the breeze from an upstairs balcony.

The conversation stays strictly within the confines of art teaching. Rani is thirsty for new ideas. She wants to know how the artist who painted a picture on the wall, did so without drawing any lines. She extracts a promise from Lorna to do some teachers' workshops despite warnings that three years' teacher training cannot be encapsulated into a couple of sessions.

Saturday April 6th

I spend a happy morning with the kids at the orphanage, who are fascinated by their photographs. I have taken picture books and a set of picture snap cards and they enjoy playing with these. A local college group has befriended them and is to supply funds to paint the place - not before time!

Ram and friends have dug down 30m to the water base and installed a pipe to pump water up to the crops – the water is very clear. I admire their enterprise. We go to lunch at Ram's house - a new building set in a field. Like many new houses there are concrete posts sticking out at the top in case the landlord wants to add a second floor. One of the Sherpas from the trek cooks a wonderful lunch. I discuss with Ram my idea for him to do a fundraising tour of England in July, staying with interested people from the trek, and he is keen to pursue this. Indeed he wants to expand the idea and bring a troupe of Nepalese dancers over with him, knowing I promote arts events. I assume his idea is that they can perform at a number of charity benefits. Knowing the amount of work involved in such an exercise I remain non-committal.

I spend the afternoon at the Aroma swimming pool, the water is not so cold this time, and I manage 12 lengths. Where all the ex-pat club members live is something of a mystery, because I rarely see them outside the club. They are very cliquey – I try to talk to them, but without success.

On my return I find I have been locked out again by the security guard who has come up with a new trick, padlocking the gate from the inside and then jumping over the wall. I retreat to Rani's for a cup of tea until the guard returns and we talk about her maternal anxieties for Jy.

Sunday April 7th
I write a song

Sarah arrives at 8.30am asking the whereabouts of her art students (I should know?) just after Nima who, having returned from his Annapurna trip, wants help to reply to an e-mail. I type out a reply. He seems put-out that I have no email facilities.

I compile masses of material for the ILO project and show it to Chandreyan before getting it photocopied. So far I have prepared everything, but feel out on a limb. I need Sunil's input to ensure that I stay on the right track, for he is the one with the lion's share of experience. The material includes song lyrics which hardly rival John Lennon but are, at least, a starting point.

The River of Shame

As a heavy flowing river
Breaks to follow separate trails

So the stories that we tell today
Form several different tales

But the source from which the stories spring
Go by the same old name

The source from which our stories flow
Is called the River of Shame

It will take a mighty effort
To divert the river's flow

But the tragic waste of human life
Demands we strike a blow

To ignore the real problem before you
Is to carry the burden of shame
But to fight exploitation of children
Can shatter the yoke and the chain.

The future demands that we win through
To do nothing is part of the crime

However small the first step, you must take it
For many there is little time

The world should look after its children
No matter how poor or what race

For to free all the young from this slavery
Advances the whole human race

If nothing else, it has supplied a title for the play: 'Rivers of Shame'.

Among the material I have produced are some guideline questions for working children, which we hope will reveal more about the children and their hopes for the future.

It is suggested I compose a parental consent letter about the project, because some of the material might shock the more traditionally-minded. I am surprised this has not already been done by the school as I would have thought this was Chandreyan's responsibility. Instead he edits the completed letter, adding extraneous information which takes it on to a second page – I persuade him eventually to leave it the way it was, but it is a struggle.

Rani has given me a task for the evening. I am to check a large pile of teachers' reports for 'inappropriate' English before they are sent to the parents. Most have pretty elaborate and fanciful turns of phrase. There is a real problem with verbosity too. I try to suggest simplicity equals elegance of style, and worry that I frequently don't achieve this myself.

Monday April 8th
Rehearsals begin

Sunil phones at 9am to say he will be two hours late, which rather scuppers my plan to give the kids a lecture about the importance of punctuality and discipline. Chandrayan, in Sunil's absence, is a useful translator when the CWIN kids arrive. I have lists drawn up for everyone, actors, researchers and backstage team. These will need revising several times as many of those originally recruited drop out as the pressure of work gets more demanding.

People stroll in late – everything is very casual – it's difficult to get them started. Chadreyan proves useful for getting order and with his help we find, redesignate and refine the lists of participants.

I outline the project and we take the children through the song lyrics. I ask for volunteers for the music group and discuss the research questions with the interviewers. I give them a pep talk about the need for self-discipline in the theatre and an opportunity to withdraw at the lunchtime session if this has given them second thoughts. Sunil arrives at 11.00am on cue for the workshops to begin and I hand over to him.

We begin some warm up exercises but progress is slow, then break into groups, allocating some of the CWIN children to each group. They are given a series of three tableaux to make, based round the four stories – the first is, the story as it is, the next is the story as it should be, the third the process by which we could get from where we are now, to where they would like the story to be. The tableaux are good and some of the solutions – women's empowerment groups in the hills for example, show a fair grasp of the issues from the sensitisation workshops.

Before we break for lunch I get a rough idea of who might be interested in acting, as opposed to backstage work. We end up with two backstage helpers for each of the four stories and discuss their roles and responsibilities.

Sunil explains his late appearance was due to a meeting with the Mayor, who has allocated Aarohan an old garment factory, as a building for a school for performing arts. Much work is needed, but they will be given the building and can raise funds for renovation. There are two large performing spaces within the building and a lot of small rooms for workshops or for visiting professionals. I tell him to book me a place.

The afternoon is largely spent defining a role for all the participants but it is an uphill struggle. I organise the research groups while Sunil takes the acting groups. We end up with three researchers to each group and I try to ensure an age mix. The three older and more serious students, who have visited

WOREC, are researching the girls' trafficking story. The brick industry seems to inspire the least interest. Some take advantage of the presence of the CWIN children who are in domestic service, to start interviewing them.

By the end of the afternoon we have four acting teams, two groups of seven and two groups of nine. Before Sunil leaves, we discuss venues for the first performance, and he suggests the Royal Nepal Academy which is a well-known, 800 seater, central venue with good lighting and acoustics. I query the cost and agree to phone the ILO in the morning to discuss the venue and the budget. If this production is to be ready for such a prestigious venue with such a big audience (I suspect we will get Government Ministers attending), we will have to work like crazy.

I retire to ask the Principal if we can arrange a visit to a brick factory – she has parents involved in the construction and brick industry. There is some irony here. I ask if they employ children, and are we going to have to be careful how we explain our 'educational' visit, but she says some of the kids involved in the ILO project come from these families, so they already know what we are doing. This is difficult for me to get my head round. We are being invited in to see children at work, when the main point of the exercise is to suggest to the owners' children that this should not be happening?

Rani has scheduled me in for English revision sessions three times a week and introduces me to Sheri, the English teacher. I am to help with revision on Shakespeare's Romeo and Juliet. I had planned to go out with Sabitha in the evening but cry off. The sky is the colour of a large bruise and the thunder is rumbling ominously. Besides, I am knackered. In bed by nine I am awake at 3.00am going over the test papers for the Shakespeare – the way they break down the text seems to be the best way to lose all spontaneity and love for the play as a piece of drama. It depresses me. I return to sleep – fitfully.

Tuesday April 9th

At 7am I am awoken by a call from Tskisi, Renu's son, talking nineteen to the dozen. I am too befuddled to concentrate. I understand he wants to come and see me at the school. 'I thought you were in India,' I say. 'I got back yesterday,' he says. He explains that he is working with a group of rag pickers and they are putting together their own street drama. For a while I think he wants to integrate them into our production but this is not the case. He asks me if we are dealing with the question of drugs. Not specifically, I say though I suspect it will be an issue. I ask if his group would like to put their drama on at Shuvatara and explain our deadlines. He thinks so. We agree to meet on Thursday and discuss this. I also ask him about interviewing the girls from WOREC and he says the students need to contact them through a related organisation, and he gives me details.

The session starts in the Hall at 9.35 am and I give the stragglers 5 minutes' grace. Twenty minutes later, Arniko, one of the more attention-seeking pupils swaggers in. I give him a dressing-down for being late. I hope I can instil a sense of urgency into them by the prospect of performing at the Royal Nepal Academy!

By the time the CWIN group arrive, we are half way through a third warm-up game. The children have obviously never done mime before and they are self-conscious. There is no sight of Nepalaya Films who are supposed to be videoing our sessions.

I get the coordinator to coax the CWIN group to join us in an exercise to develop tonal qualities in the voice. I demonstrate to all of them what I want them to do and they are clearly startled by my voice projection. Arniko mimics me. I make a mental note. He is a clever mimic, has a loud voice and needs watching in more ways than one.

The CWIN children work in a group of three because the youngest, Kusum, is only ten and very shy. It is mainly the CWIN girls that seem reticent. Most of the CWIN lads have strong voices and a confident stage presence, which is far beyond my expectations. What is really striking is their quiet maturity. They are outnumbered, in an unfamiliar setting, yet they exude a calm assurance. It is quite remarkable.

Some of the older, more conscientious school children throw themselves enthusiastically into the work. Despite their inexperience they seem motivated, have expressive voices and will be very useful members of the group. They take direction quickly and intelligently, and unlike some of the younger children they are not afraid to lose themselves in a characterisation.

I am aware however of potentially disruptive and unserious elements in the group. I think it is because some of the school children are very self-conscious about the issues, though I should not discount normal adolescent behaviour!

After lunch, we try out three scenarios for improvisations. These are:-

- Unmarried daughter returns home pregnant.
- Father arrives home drunk - family try and placate him as he has a tendency to turn violent .
- Father has arranged a marriage for daughter, daughter opposes it and so does her mother, but she will not stand up to the father.

We ask them to create a scene around the issues and also to round it to some conclusion. On reflection, I ask the Shuvatara children to do it in Nepali and then repeat it in English for my benefit. This turns out to be unnecessary. The unmarried daughter sketch is so graphic I don't need a translation, I can easily gauge their acting skills. Arniko has obviously supplied lots of the ideas and direction for his group and puts in a strong performance. Sang Kalpa makes a fearsome Nepali Aunt who wants to throw the girl out, Pukar a good strong father figure. Poor Megha gets the short straw as the pregnant daughter and slumps on her chair helplessly most of the time. They make good use of the stage and enjoy themselves.

In the second group Shirjit makes a very credible drunk, but he is playing for laughs. His manner is supposed to terrorise his family but this drunk wouldn't terrorise a current bun. He needs to connect with the underlying serious issues. None of them have gone below the surface yet. Early days, early days.

The CWIN group are confident with their story – they are on familiar territory. I am delighted when little Kusum, the 'arranged' daughter, comes forward and gives 'dad' a talking to – there is a gentle, acknowledging clap. We must build her in a small part. I note she has mentioned she wants to be a dancer when she is older, maybe we can use that.

I retire to the school office to make various arrangements. Rani's son Jy has been slotted into the music group. Later, over tiffin, Rani talks about the problems of parenthood again. We discuss the possibility of Jy taking a year out after 'O' Levels. He is interested in nature, so I suggest sending him on a conservation project where he can't get into trouble and has time to grow up and fend for himself. I have somewhere like Africa in mind, but Rani thinks Chitwan is the right place but worries that he will get in with girl tourists and their 'loose, pot-smoking ways'. I think this might be shutting the door after the horse has bolted – he has, after all, spent a year in Oz. I think Jy probably needs to be somewhere where money and privilege count for nothing, where he has to stand on his own feet and no one rescues him from his mistakes. I don't know if Rani is ready to let him take those risks.

Wednesday April 10th
The Kumari

Punctuality is still a problem, with the added complication that new people have turned up wanting to join in and some of the original group don't turn up. We follow the same format as yesterday. We have some potentially strong performers and, despite the shyness and self-consciousness, some of the scenes are played with perception and intelligence.

I phone the ILO to find no one has done anything about the venue. Bimal wishes to pass the problem to Sunil who he says he can negotiate a better price. I point out that if we don't know what they have got in the budget and don't know the venues available, surely the first job is to check that. I suggest that he or Aditee phone potential venues for availability checks. I give them the dates we would need for a dress rehearsal, technical and performance. I don't know yet what implications this has for the school exams. Our project does not appear to be co-ordinated or thought through in the way I would hope, given the timescale we are working to.

I meet Sabitha in town. She is late, then just when I think I will have to walk home, suddenly she is there with her lovely warm smile. We go to New Road to see if my photographs are ready, but come away empty-handed – there are technical problems.

Sabitha then tours me round the New Road / Freak Street area I have seen only fleetingly. Even encrusted with dirt, the carved wooden shutters and balconies of the houses are magnificent. It looks as if some of the shops are still hoping to cater for latter-day hippies, because we pass several selling bell-bottomed loons covered in psychedelic flowers. They look awful - did we really wear those things? Some are so old that the sun has faded them, and some are covered in thick dust.

Sabitha cuts through an alley suddenly and points to an ugly run-down concrete building in a back courtyard. She tells me this is where Shyam's grandmother lives. It is in stark contrast to her grandson's home. 'You know her then?' I ask. She does. It seems Rani (whom she calls 'auntie') took her and her brother there for visits when they were little.

Sabitha tells me her father died when she was five months old and her mother, who teaches cookery, brought her and Ashok up alone. Their house backs on to the school, indeed was there before the school – Shuvatara sort of grew up round them. Befriended by the Kakshapatis, it is not surprising that they should both end up working for them.

From Freak Street we turn up into Basantapur Square where many of the monuments date back to the 12th century. We pass the old Royal Palace which is an architectural delight of variegated brickwork and superb wood carvings, including a depiction of the gods surround by frantic erotic scenes!

At the west end of the square Sabitha points out the building that houses the young girl chosen to serve as the Royal Kumari. This is another example of the bizarre enslavement of a child in the name of a religious tradition that dates back to at least the 15th century. The Kumari is a young Buddhist Newar virgin who is worshipped as the incarnation of the Hindu goddess Durga. While there are a dozen minor Kumaris worshipped throughout the valley there is only one Royal Kumari. The minor ones attend a few festivals but otherwise lead relatively normal lives, but this is not the case for the Royal Kumari who leads a regimented life holed up in this richly decorated house on Durbar Square.

Her appointment is bizarre. She is selected after a search by high priests for likely candidates among the young girls of the Shakya caste – she is expected to have certain attributes, 'eyelashes like a cow' and 'a neck like a conch shell'! Those that make the shortlist are put in a dark room filled with bloody buffalo heads, and the one that doesn't freak out in this chamber of horrors reveals herself as embodying the fierce goddess Durga. If her horoscope also passes the test, she is then ritually installed and cared for daily by attendants, who deck her out in red robes and all kinds of finery, paint black kohl around her eyes, and leave her to a strange life of receiving devotees and having high priests worship her once a day.

Since her restlessness during a puja is taken as a bad omen she is also expected to suppress her normal childish instincts during acts of worship. Outside this she can play with the children of the attendants but she does not go to school and cannot play outside the building because her feet must not touch the ground. On the rare occasions she leaves the building, she is carried by attendants.

When she starts menstruating or if she sheds blood – a scratch is enough – the god is believed to leave her body and she is replaced and sent home with a small stipend from the state. There is, however, a superstition that the husbands of Kumari die young, so she will not find it easy to acquire a husband – an abnormal state in Nepal. Since most parents don't want a long-term illiterate and unwed daughter on their hands for the sake of a few years' fame and glory, there has been a marked reduction of candidates for the honour in recent years, though I would hope that for some parents the idea of incarcerating a small child might also be a deterrent.

Sabitha then takes me to a favourite spot, the ancient bead bazaar by Indra Chowk, a glittering mass of tiny, open stalls where the shimmering hues of multi-coloured beads hanging in profusion are absolutely dazzling.

By 8pm she is anxious to return home. This is not surprising in the present climate, but Nepalis generally show a preference for early nights and equally early mornings. The erratic power supply probably reinforces that pattern. I tell her my daughters often don't go out till 10.30pm. I can see she thinks I am exaggerating.

Thursday April 11th
Rajan's Story

We have a meeting with the instrumentalists (minus their instruments) and Anju, who has been roped in as a vocalist, to create music for the opening song. I note that so far we have one violinist, a flute and keyboard player, two on drums and percussion, two on electric bass guitar and one rhythm guitar, one set of congas and two madal players. Raj Dulal from CWIN, arrives twenty minutes after the others. He, at least, has brought his madal so we are able to hear him play – he's very good.

Raj's own story as a rag picker has been researched, typed, and submitted by Abhash, one of the older Shuvatara pupils – it's disturbing but also moving because of what Abhash writes in conclusion.

Raj was born into a poor farmer's family in a remote village in Chitwan. His mother had two children, Raj and an older brother, but his father then took a second wife and had another eight children by her. Raj's mother left home after she was severely beaten by his drunken father. She left both her young children with the stepmother, who deliberately mistreated and malnourished them until Raj also ran away from home at the age of seven.

Penniless, he somehow made his way to Kathmandu where an uncle put him to work selling peanuts in the street.

Raj fell ill but his uncle and other relatives did nothing to help him, so he ran away again and began life on the streets, rag picking, stealing, begging. Sometimes he was lucky and earned as much as 100-150 rupees in a day – about 50p – sometimes he earned nothing. He was introduced to drugs, accused of stealing and beaten severely. Eventually he was found by CWIN and offered an alternative. He now lives in one of their hostels. He has no idea what has happened to his parents. He is fourteen, thin as a rake and has the worn face of someone four times his age.

Abhash wrote at the end of his account on Raj 'What has happened in his 14 years can't be changed and I guess no commiseration can be of any help. But I would just like to know who is to blame for all this. I somewhat feel like, is it us?'… I feel we are on the verge of some kind of breakthrough.

Back in the staffroom everyone is frantically collating marks for the end of term and I am roped in to correct more reports. All the young Grade One teachers come for a meeting with Rani in wonderful, brightly-coloured new saris to celebrate the New Year – they look like vivid butterflies. In the centre of the school an extra storey is being added to the Vice-Principal's Office and the Stationery Stores. The workmen in turbans and longi are incredibly thin and move in a slow, deliberate way. One man looks as if he has rickets.

Friday April 12th
The price of bricks

Surprisingly almost everyone is on time except the CWIN kids, who swing onto the bus just as we are leaving. The brick factory we are going to is in a place called Lobo, Sanagou and the company is called The Karnamay Chimney Bhata. I understand it is owned by one of the parents. This makes the visit a little awkward.

We climb up a hill off the ring road into a semi-rural landscape and then it is there to the left – an extraordinary sight – acres of the valley cut into grey islands of clay, each one surrounded by water-filled trenches and a sea of raw grey bricks laid out to dry in the sun in endless rows. In the middle are two chimneys belching out grey smoke.

The sight that meets me as I get off the bus, is like something out of the Dark Ages. A cluster of small children, mainly girls, the oldest can be no more than five, watch us curiously. They are filthy, their clothes are encrusted with clay, their hair is matted. Many have small nose rings. One child, who is about two, is encrusted all over and her head is shaved. Behind her stands a boy with a cloth on his head. I would guess he is between twelve and fourteen (making allowances for the fact that working children are much smaller), and covered from head to toe in brick dust. He is carrying eight rows of bricks on his head. His bare legs are skeletal and he is wearing only flip-flops on his feet. Another small child with a doca (porter's basket) attached to his forehead is down in a trench having the basket filled with bricks. Two young women pass us and I count thirty-six bricks strapped to their backs on ropes attached by a band to their forehead.

The manager, who does not speak English, takes the students across the site to where a young woman is kneading damp clay into a wooden mould – just as you might knead bread. Several of the jokers in the pack decide to have a go at making bricks, but somehow I cannot share their enthusiasm for 'mud pie making'. They don't seem to have got the message that this is someone's living and that we are disrupting their work. Later, I ask the pupils to find out the daily rate – estimates vary from 80 rupees (80p) to 225 rupees (£2.25) – the amount I have paid for a drink in a tourist hotel. These workers turn out up to 1,200 bricks in a day for that amount.

I want to break through the school kids' frivolity by making them do a calculation to underline the seriousness of the situation:-

'You have just made 4 bricks in 20 minutes – three of them are unusable. That's a rate of 3 useable bricks in an hour. Assuming an average rate of 150 rupees for 1,200 bricks, how long would you have to work to earn this much?'

I think I make that 400 hours. The workers here produce that many in a day. I ask how long it takes for the bricks to dry completely. The answer is five days and the manager confirms that, if it rains in that time, the bricks are ruined. The ILO reports suggest that when this happens it is the workforce that bears the loss in their wages. Can you imagine? Seeing 5 days' backbreaking work for which you have earned the princely sum of £7.50 disappear in front of your eyes, no compensation – no retainer.

I watch a young woman with the wrinkles of an old lady shovel dry dust into a sack. A tiny child, wearing only a small vest clings to her. I ask if I may photograph him. I feel self-conscious and awkward asking, but have a need to document what I am seeing, in case, later, I think I only imagined it.

In the distance are some huts made of raw bricks and covered with straw. The top of the thatched roof comes only to my shoulder. Two tiny grubby children stand by the entrance, which is just an uncovered opening. I take their photograph. There is a smell of cooking inside. Apart from the doorway, the shelter is unventilated. The atmosphere is thick with dust and smoke. The children all seem to have coughs and snot running down their noses. One or two have half-closed, infected eyes. There appears to be no proper sanitation on site. I look around in vain for even a water tap. There is none. Water for cooking must come from the trenches.

We walk over and climb up the crumbling embankment by the chimneys.

The area in front of the chimneys is very hot and there are rows of small, metal lids set into the ground with smoke coming out of them. The heat is piped underground to small ovens where the bricks are baked. I understand this work is allocated to the Indian workers because the Nepalis cannot cope with the heat. There seems to be a subtle hierarchy between the two workforces.

I climb down the other embankment because I want to photograph some young boys carrying bricks, but they turn away. A woman worker approaches me talking very rapidly and aggressively. It is obvious she wants money. I feel terrible. I would happily give her money, but what about all the others?

A man, seeing my interest in children, picks up a tiny baby who starts to cry. He forces the baby's head round so that I can photograph it, presumably because he is expecting a payment, and the boys who have been walking away now pose in a line balancing the bricks on their heads. One stands on one leg as if he was a circus performer. I put the camera away. I feel ashamed, embarrassed and deeply upset that I have raised their expectations unfairly. How can I possibly explain my motives - what would I say even if I could speak their language? I find Anju and ask her to come back and act as translator but she cannot understand the woman – 'She is Indian,' she says.

The Shuvatara pupils are back by the bus. 'Can we go now, Miss?' asks Arniko the mud pie maker. I look at him: tall, good looking, expensively and casually dressed, the over-confident child of rich parents, who has come here, had a few laughs with his mates and now wants to go back because he is bored. I am having trouble controlling my feelings. I try and distract myself by asking the manager the significance of the small rubber discs in a metal bucket being carried by one of the workers. I am told these are tokens that are later changed into cash when a quota of bricks is finished.

As we are getting ready to leave, the owner says something to the bus driver who seems to know him well. I understand that he has called for a crate of drinks for the visitors. I watch two labourers carrying down crates of drinks into the site. I cannot bear it.

In front of the disbelieving stares of dozens of tiny, filthy children lined up to watch these healthy, clean, well-dressed children, this man passes up bottles of Fanta, Sprite and Coke to the kids in the bus. I have asked myself a million times since, why I did not intervene before the bottles entered the bus and ask for the drinks to be given instead to the child workers. It would have been the correct thing to do. I can only conclude I was in a state of shock and shame and certain in the knowledge that this request would be refused. Instead I ask to pay for them. The manager declines. I do not accept a drink, I think it will choke me. How can they drink in front of these other children?

We are like visitors from another planet so vast is the divide. When did those dirty little illiterate children who make such a disproportionate contribution to the prosperity of this business ever get offered a crate of drinks by their boss, who spends the fruits of their labour sending his child to a private school far away from their wildest dreams and expectations. I am also conscious of the fact that, though they may assist their parents, most of these little children will not even be included in the statistics of child labourers because they are not directly employed.

As the children finish their drinks, a large, traditionally-dressed lady boards the bus together with another, tiny, elderly woman. I understand they want a lift to Sanepa. As the bus pulls out, I ask Anju once more to translate for me and I find that this woman lives opposite the brick factory, is concerned about the condition of the children on the site and wants to start a school for them. She is retired but used to work for an NGO. She gives me her telephone number. Perhaps there is something we can do to help

The school she proposes would be for young children and I try and find out from her at what age the children on the site are considered part of the workforce and given heavy weights to carry. I am told, and the pupils later confirm this, that no one will talk about the age factor but will only say that it depends on the size of the child. I doubt any ILO Convention rules and regulations determines what is appropriate. I ask the woman how many children there are on site. I am told 36. When I query the low number, I am told the rest are Indians and have not been counted.

I ask Anju about the distinction between the Indians and the Nepalis and whether this is just due to a language barrier. She says 'no' because there is no one language among the Indians anyway – they come from many different regions and they have to understand Nepali to understand the supervisors. I recognise I am getting into the intricacies of the caste system.

I look around the bus. Apart from Anju and one or two of the more thoughtful girls, the rest are in high spirits and making a hell of a racket. The CWIN group are significantly detached and very, very silent. I ask Anju to ask Raju what he thought of the visit. He says he was very depressed seeing children living like that and that something should be done about it. Raju is 14. He has had his own troubles, he is the same age as Arniko but he could not be more different in his reactions. I convey how much I agree with him.

On our return from school I accost Arniko as he is about to cycle off on his mountain bike to ask what he thought of the visit. 'It was great, Miss,' he says. I am dumbfounded. 'Great?' I don't know what distresses me more, what I have seen today, or the reactions of these wealthy kids to the visit. For they will be the next generation with power in this country.

In the late afternoon I meet Rita for a final goodbye. She is at a Peace rally called by the Human Rights Solidarity for Peace. It is a tiny turnout. I tell her about the brick site visit. She comments that most of the bricks produced in this manner are of such poor quality that, if Nepal experiences another earthquake, and given the freakish weather we have been suffering that does not seem beyond the bounds of possibility, most of the buildings constructed with them are likely to be reduced to dust.

Rita needs presents to take home and I accompany her, but I am not in the mood after a day like today. The faces of those kids at the brickworks still haunt me.

The reception committee ©Photograph H Roy

The visitors©Photograph H Roy

Saturday April 13th
Nepalese New Year's Eve

At Midnight we celebrate 2059 – the Nepali Vedic calendar is 56.7 years ahead of ours. I should live so long! By contrast I spend the day writing up the brick site visit.

The Kakshapati's party is at the International Club. I am summoned early to help arrange flowers. The club looks impressive considering that behind some of the drapes there is still a virtual building site. Multi-coloured flowers have been mass planted at short notice in the surrounding gardens. In the inner courtyard a team of didis are scrubbing the tiling in the empty swimming pool.

As evening draws in, fairy lights illuminate the flowers and the trees. On either side of the imposing entrance are big brass pitchers full of exotic red and orange flowers and aromatic oil burns in brass receptacles. Visitors are adorned with red tikka spots as they enter and waiters offer tiny terra-cotta saucers of Nepalese fortified wine. The taste is very earthy, like a cross between Calvados and Arak.

Rani looks very glamorous. By comparison I look like a washed-out missionary, but find it bothers me little. All the glitterati from Kathmandu seem to be here. I am the only European. Many of the women look formidable matriarchs.

A good R&B band provides me with the opportunity to fling myself into the dancing which takes place inside the empty swimming pool, which is quaint. I need to lose myself in some concentrated exercise, to the delight of some and the clear disapproval of others. Exposure to the two extremes of Nepali society within 24 hours has been hard to take.

I walk back sobered by the thought, and comfortably alone. It has been the first social evening I have experienced in Nepal that finished after midnight and with many of the familiar conventions of New Year. I am aware I have more in common with the people at the event tonight in terms of my standard of living back home, but the experience of Friday has made me feel detached from this world of comfort and pleasure. I am aware I do not fit in here, either.

Sunday April 14th
Pessimism and picnics

Today I meet Ram who helps me arrange a weekend visit to the Chitwan National Park in the Terai. This could be my last chance to see the region. Outside the travel office a massive chariot is under construction, the size of the Trojan horse. This is the centrepiece of next Saturday's Festival of Machhendranath, Lord of the Fishes, the patron protector of the valleys.

After I leave Ram, I cycle to Lorna's. She has invited me over for a meal with Sarah at her guesthouse. Lorna is married to a Sherpa, but they live separately. She tells me about her trekking business and her farm back home in Lancashire. Her husband spends much of his time now in London, but as they are still married, Lorna is able to stay in Nepal for extended periods. The guest house owner is stationed in Hong Kong. The rent is modest, as she maintains the property. She is concerned about the political situation and the effect on tourism and believes a civil war is imminent.

I tell her about Ram's orphanage. Her comment is that there are hundreds of small welfare organisations milking foreigners and grant aid bodies for money, but little goes to the recipients. I respect her experience and understand her cynicism but feel myself resisting it. I also have good reason to be pessimistic about human nature. But it is balanced by hope. I have had days and nights when I felt life was hardly worth living, but there are also times when amazing things happen and I am carried along by them – one needs to be open to that basic enthusiasm for life, for there can be no colour and warmth, and no real change without it.

I don't feel that enthusiasm in Lorna or Sarah. Yet they are both artists and have a good eye. It seems in contrast to this critical pessimism within them. You have to believe in people – not unrealistically or without awareness, but if you are always looking for things to criticise you will surely find them. They act as if they have all the answers – I am the first to admit I have very few. Lorna thinks I should not have gone on the peace rally either, because 'you don't know who is behind it'. She may have a point. I must seem hopelessly naive to her.

I am given a tour of the house. The neighbourhood has the usual full, rich social mix. The owner of the San Miguel beer company lives opposite in a lavish villa. Next door there are teachers, and at the rear of the house a small shanty town of makeshift shacks. The residents sell their cauliflowers to the neighbours.

It is my turn to be questioned about my motivation for coming to Nepal. I am drawn out rather more than I intended and find my host has had her moments picking through the emotional wreckage too. Do women with heartache gravitate to Nepal?

We talk about the child labour project and she says she is not against child labour, which rather takes me aback, as she does not qualify this. I think there is a distinction between children assisting their families in order to survive, and out and out child exploitation. Ranged against that is the dialectic of global capitalism which militates against removing children as the cheapest form of labour. International mandates will have little impact on poor children and their families without a social structure which upholds citizens' rights.

What is needed in places like Nepal, India and much of Africa is sustained economic development. It is what rescued Victorian working-class children from being sent down mines and up chimneys. We should not allow ourselves to believe it is part of the culture and therefore we have to accept it as inevitable. I am sure Lorna would not want to see any child of hers in the brick sites I have visited.

By contrast my host has strong feelings about the treatment of dogs and introduces me to a rather neurotic but magnificent black mastiff that, I am told, was ill-treated by a previous neighbour. When Lorna left she stole the dog. He looks at me with suspicion and growls softly.

My host's other visitor arrives. Jodie comes from Perth, has been living here for seven years and works at the Dwarika, a showcase hotel near Pushapatinath. The hotel was built along traditional lines by an architect wishing to preserve the old traditional Newari building techniques.

Her job has quite a lot of outreach aspects, one of which is the 'Clean up the Bagmati River project'. That will take a lifetime, I think. Affectionately known as 'the sewer of the valley' the stink of shit as you pass over any of the bridges is unmistakeable. At present it is a toxic cocktail of solid waste, sewage, sludge, industrial effluents, cremation ashes and animal carcasses mixed with some water. No wonder that the number of pilgrims to Pushapatinath prepared to bathe in the sacred waters has been declining.

As she talks about her latest feasibility proposals to Lorna, who is on the same committee, I realise my ex-lover is one of their advisors, not that surprising, given his work field is the international conservation of sacred sites. I feared I would stumble over someone who knew him sooner or later. Jodie met him when he was over here with a colleague and has been trying to contact both of them recently without any success. I look at all her submissions – I wonder if they will ever get beyond the feasibility stage?

Later, over dinner, she asks me about the International Club manager's post, having heard the Nanglo chain have taken the club over again. This is a job Rani asked me if I would be interested in, an enquiry I had not taken seriously because I felt the job required a native Nepali speaker. Jodie does not apparently consider this a necessity. In the seven years she has been in Nepal she has not found the inclination to learn the language. However she then surprises me by saying she would not consider the post unless they were paying a European, as opposed to a local salary.

I seem to recall a recent conversation about people who live out here for next to nothing, still expecting large salaries. I try and visualise a Nepali walking into Claridges and informing the owners (in Nepali) that he is prepared to consider managing the hotel but has no intention of learning English and will only consider the job if the salary is doubled.

Monday April 15th
Visa renewal day

I leave early. I got cold feet last night about crossing the city in the dark on a bicycle with all the curfews imposed. Lorna put me up with barely disguised reluctance but I have already outstayed my welcome.

I cycle through the misty, early morning air, which is the best time to be on a bike in Kathmandu. I get lost, and arrive at the visa office 15 minutes before the opening time of 9.00am which is notional anyway, as no one arrives to attend to us till 9.30am. In the present climate business is understandably slack. There are only two others waiting to renew visas, a Japanese student and a middle-aged woman who has the washed-out complexion I associate with one who has devoted their life to God and good works.

I part with fifty dollars and am told to return at 4pm to collect my passport. I call into the ILO offices on my way back. I am concerned that a week has gone by and the ILO doesn't appear to have found us a venue for the play. Rita warned me before her departure that Bimal is about to leave the country to work in Belgium, but I phoned him yesterday and he did not mention it.

Bimal deftly dodges my attempts to pin him down about the venue but does locate the film crew, who were apparently waiting for a schedule from us before they came to film rehearsals. When he excuses himself citing a meeting, I ask his colleague if it is true he is leaving soon to live in Belgium. 'Oh yes,' she says, 'this is his last day in the office.' I am staggered. I have been talking to the guy for the best part of an hour and he has failed to mention that he is relinquishing the project, and has walked out without even saying goodbye. Anju promises to contact the venues and arranges for a school visit to a brick factory in Bhaktapur the following day. Our previous brick site visit was so traumatic we gained no interviews, only a pictorial record and we need to properly interview some young brick workers.

I ring the school to check that transport can be provided. Rani wants to know where I am and why I can't come on the school picnic. It seems the school is decamping to King Tribhuvan Memorial Park in Thankot on the Pokhara road. I never seem to pick these things up in advance on the bush telegraph. She insists Sunil should be left in charge of rehearsals. I leave Anju with the promise that a Mrs Shiva Shrestha, will meet us at the gates of Bhaktapur hospital at 9.30am tomorrow to guide us to the brick site. 'Is there only one hospital in Bhaktapur?' I ask suspiciously. She assures me there is.

I get back to find Chandreyan in holiday mood. 'Come on the picnic,' he booms and offers a lift on his motorbike. When I see how much of the journey is uphill I am pleased I have agreed. The journey is also useful as I am able to ask him about the ILO budget, which he had a hand in compiling. I am staggered to discover the overall grant is 2 rak (200,000 rupees – that's £2,000 – a fortune out here – and that does not include Sunil's fee!) I ask him how he sees this money being spent as the venue costs will be 45,000 rupees at the most, and with all the production costs allowed for, we will, by my calculation, have spent only 30% of the budget. The only additional item he has allowed for, unsurprisingly, is food. What is to happen to the surplus? It would distress me if the money were to 'disappear' when CWIN could do such useful work with it. I resolve to try and keep track of all expenditure.

Tribhuvan Park is in the shadow of the mountain range. A long set of central steps lead up to a giant statue of the King. I ask Chandreyan when the king reigned but he says he is no good at history. I later find Tribhuvan is a relatively contemporary 20th Century monarch. The park is large and strewn with rubbish – the aftermath of New Year's Day picnics. Some desultory attempts are being made to clear it by two attendants with forks and baskets, but aside from the rubbish being burned in large cement bins, the surplus seems to have been chucked over a bank into a stream, adding seriously to the water pollution in the area. Apart from the burning rubbish, dozens of barbecues contribute to the smoky atmosphere. The park stretches uphill towards the mountains. If you can ignore the debris, this is a beautiful and inspiring place. The blend of spiritual beauty and squalor epitomises Nepal.

We find the Shuvatara staff installed in a metal, two-tier shelter – there are a number in the park, full of picnickers. The school have laid out carpets on the ground floor, calor gas cookers are set up and a barbecue is on the go. Judging by the quantities of food, cooks, washers up, saucepans, bowls and crates of drink they have brought, it looks as if they have set up residence for a week. I am plied with meat from the barbecue until I remind them I don't eat it, when the choice of food shrinks dramatically to puffed rice, horseradish pickle and a plate of carrot and cucumber. Later a plate of Daal Bhat appears.

This is a popular event. Upstairs a ghetto blaster pumps out Nepali music, several staff have brought guitars and madals and I am roped in to join the dancing. Rani seems relaxed and happy and sings some Nepali folk tales. I manage to slip in the information about my meeting with Bimal and the large surplus on the budget. She finds Bimal's behaviour extraordinary too.

I leave while the celebrations are in full flood to recover my passport. Rani arranges for her driver to take me back down to the ring road where I can get a cab into town. The driver pulls up in a brand new Cadillac I have not seen before. Despite the slump, the Kakshapati's are obviously prospering. Rani says the school is full to overflowing and they now have a long waiting list, while all the other schools are advertising like mad for new pupils.

The passport is ready – they have hardly had a rush on, but when I get back to the school there is no sign of Sunil and the hall is locked up. I phone him later and he explains they were late starting, not all of them turned up, and then they said they had to leave early to catch their bus. I think they are wrapping him round their little finger. I say I will be there by 12 tomorrow for a meeting with the film crew – I have suggested they talk to Sunil alone, but they insist they want to talk to me, which is crazy because Sunil is much more experienced than I am.

I phone the ILO because Anju has left me a message about the cost of the respective halls, but not their availability. We talk at cross-purposes until I discover she is under the misconception we have received the first instalment of the grant for the project and can book the hall ourselves. I thought Chandreyan was co-ordinating this project?

Further problems arise when Ashok, sent to get the cheque, delivers it to the school accountant and there is a bit of a battle between me and the accountant as I try to explain that it is not school money and has to be set aside for our project. He looks at me darkly and holds the cheque at arm's length with distaste as if it is a large dog turd. The amount I note is for 110,000 rupees.

I stay up writing late and then lie awake worrying about whether we are going to pull this off. I feel OK about leaving Sunil to progress the work as I have done the majority of the planning and preparation so far. But I have to remember he has many other commitments, so I should not be surprised if he is unable to put this project centre stage.

Tuesday April 16th
Research into action - I write a play

Transport for the four of us going to the brick factory has been arranged for 8.30am but we are not on the road till shortly after 9. The driver pulls out all the stops to get us to Bhaktapur by 9.30am. We swing into the hospital grounds and park up dead on time. We wait. We wait some more. The drivers wanders off. I phone Anju only to discover we are looking for a man not a woman – how stupid of me – of course Shiva is a male name. I ask what our Shiva looks like. I am told he has dark hair and skin and is 5ft 7. She has just described about 95% of the male population of Nepal. A further half an hour goes by and we finally locate our man. He has been waiting at another set of gates. Just before 11.00am we relocate the driver and set off, passing a second hospital on the way. Things could have been worse – Shiva could have been waiting at that one.

We arrive late at the brick site, but we would never have found it without a guide. It is much larger than the other site we visited. There are the same small, workers' huts dotted about the site, but there is running water here. We are taken to a small building in the middle of the site and up some crude concrete stairs into a small office. This is the base for the Child Development Society and Shiva explains they organise health and hygiene education, as well as run a small day centre for the younger children.

There is a supply of medicines on a hot window ledge. They are covered in dust, and the cardboard boxes are beginning to curl. I discover they cannot distribute the drugs because the promised health centre has yet to materialise. The drugs look as if they will be well past their use-by date before they are dispensed. I note vitamin A pills are among the store. A national report by CWIN last year found 3,000 children a year die in Nepal from diseases caused by simple Vitamin A deficiency.

Time is ticking on. Eventually three little boys appear, between the ages of about 5 and 11. I am relieved to see that they are significantly cleaner than the children we saw on Friday. While the Shuvatara girls talk to the boys I go and photograph the little children in the day centre who are at first coy and then end up clamouring to be in each picture. Suddenly three girls from the brick site are ushered in and it seems worthwhile to stay a little longer, since they have been kind enough to leave their work to talk to us.

Later the pupils share their findings with me. Two of the girl workers are from Rolpa, a district in West Nepal with a strong Maoist base. Now fourteen and fifteen they have been coming to work at the brick site for two years. Their brother has sent them to do this work. They earn between 5-6000 rupees a month, which averages at about 40p per day. One has reached Class 2 standard and one Class 3 at school – the grades for a 7 or 8 year old. They complain of back pain and carry 28 bricks at a time. They would both like to be at home but have been driven back to the site each year by poverty. We get no information about the third girl.

For the first time we find a lad who seemed moderately satisfied with his job. He has never been to school. After Friday's visit, this trip is mildly reassuring in the sense that, however inadequate, there is at least the presence of an outside agency on the site to monitor, inform and give very small children a chance to escape for a few hours. The more I think of it, the more it suggests to me that this story should be about a whole family rather than one individual because of the way the work impacts on the life of the whole group. Although there are plenty of individual workers here we have got too little to frame a whole story around them.

We are late getting back and the film crew are patiently waiting. We discuss what has been done so far and what they might film in the rehearsals. I point out that we are unlikely to get a strong story line developing till the end of the week, but there are some themes emerging:-

Background of children

A common background of poverty – the children are either from farms in the hills, Chitwan or the surrounding Terai. One has an urban background and a father who was a hospital peon – many have lost parents either through death or disappearance. Indeed that is the second common theme.

Family disruption.

One piece of research revealed this story – it is not uncommon. The boys' father, who was an alcoholic, married a second wife; the first wife was beaten till she ran away abandoning her children to the stepmother. The children of the first wife were abused and beaten by the stepmother who deprived them of food. The father was too drunk to care. The abuse was so considerable they too ran away. The brothers have lost contact with each other.

In another story, the mother died in childbirth, the father died of alcoholism, and no relatives were able to afford to keep the children.

We also have the harrowing account of an older sister who was sold to a brothel by her relatives. The younger sisters joined their brother at the brick sites to protect them from the traffickers after their parents died. The older sister has disappeared.

In another life story, the mother eloped and the father abandoned his daughter. Her grandparents took her in but treated her like a slave.

The migration of the whole family due to poverty is another theme. The health of the whole family declined in the brick yards, affecting their ability to work – a vicious cycle of malnutrition and sickness.

Work experience

Researchers found a 10 year old who worked as a domestic from 5am to midnight with no salary, only food and clothes. She was thrown out when she left the house, without permission, to buy tea for visitors who had asked her to perform this errand. She was found wandering in Ratna Park by representatives from CWIN. Luckily they found her before the traffickers.

One boy was a peanut seller at 10 years, then a rag picker and pickpocket. He turned to drugs and was beaten severely by the police when accused of stealing.

One brick worker who started work at six years old and is now twelve, works a 14 hour day earning 3000 rupees (approx £1.50) a day. He carries ten bricks at a time, suffers from neck and back pain, breathing problems, skin rashes, nightmares, insomnia, anxiety and depression. He has no medical care and is abused by adult workers.

Situation now

The domestic is at a CWIN hostel, learning sewing. The rag picker is in CWIN found accommodation and wants to train to teach dance. The brick worker is still at the site – now with his younger sisters and cannot afford to leave. Intermediaries take 10% of his salary.

Family connections severed

The domestic has no connections – only unhappy memories of abandonment. The rag picker has lost contact with his mother and brother and has no contact with the father and stepmother who abused him. The brick worker's parents and uncle are all dead – he is now responsible for his younger sisters. His older sister is in a brothel.

Solutions – such as they are:

- Strengthen the work of the NGOs
- Increase the inspectorate
- Conduct programme of public awareness starting in schools
- Improve the superstructure in farming communities
- Encourage village committees, children's clubs, empowerment groups in rural areas
- Extend education to illiterate adults – literate parents place more value on education for children (research suggests high connection between illiteracy of parents and non-attendance at school by children)
- Develop controlled family education in villages on trafficking – provide help with health education, education and financial self-sufficiency
- Implement fines and imprisonment for the abuse of minors
- Strengthen international co-operation against paedophile rings and sex industry traffickers
- Provide subsidies for small manufacturers to employ adults, not children (research by the ILO suggests that a 5-10% increase in the prices of finished goods would be sufficient subsidy to pay the extra for an adult worker)
- Improve adult wages
- Research and boycott goods abroad produced by child labour. Support

the purchase of goods with logos which show they have been produced without child labour. Run local campaigns in the developed world to increase public awareness

- Create government targets for improvements in literacy, health and working conditions
- Create awareness programmes to focus on the culture of abuse and to challenge traditional notions such as 'a girl's duty'
- Government action is needed on gender discrimination, caste and racial discrimination

General thoughts / conclusions from research so far

Nepal treats its cows better than its children. Cows can roam where they like, can feed where they like and are venerated. Why are the young not equally respected and venerated?

Some of the most shocking facts must be brought out:-

- Children are tortured with salt and chilli poured into their eyes if they fall asleep
- Paedophile rings on the internet in the US, UK and Australia tell paedophiles where they can target children for abuse in the developing countries
- Children are deliberately blinded and maimed to provide a living as beggars
- Children are infected with syphilis and AIDS
- Children are sold into bonded slavery, imprisoned and hidden by traffickers
- Children are sold for their organs

We have to highlight that the trade in human trafficking is 10 times higher than the Transatlantic slave trade at its height. How many people realise that? It is one of the most shocking statistics we have been given by the ILO.

I explain to the film makers that I do not know how we can accommodate all this information but these are the kinds of stories, issues and concerns I would like us to tackle. They are coming back to film the rehearsals tomorrow. I am concerned, however, that I should not be presented as an expert.

Sunil has been moving on from yesterday's improvisations that explored the working child's background, to those focusing on the child as a labourer or in an exploitative situation. Tomorrow we want to develop improvisations to explore how working children see their future.

One group is trailing behind due to a disruptive pupil dominating the proceedings and Sunil's reluctance to act as a disciplinarian. I finally tell Rani and she tells me the lad is on parole at Shuvatara having been kicked out of another school for being impossible.

We start rehearsals but it is so intensely hot that by 3.30pm I have to call a halt as no one is concentrating. The sun is beating down on the tin roof of the hall and the fans have proved ineffectual. Nepalaya wants to interview me now even though I am hot, sweaty and must look an absolute wreck, so we find an empty classroom. The interview goes as well as can be expected, but I feel I am at the borders of my knowledge and hope it comes across better than I think.

Wednesday April 17th

Today we start at 8.30am looking at the research done on sex trafficking and the rag pickers story. Probalta has managed to interview one girl, but when her group start preparing the improvisation based on the interview, I think some of the details must have been manufactured it seems so full of melodrama. I suggest that they stick to the real story. It turns out this is the real story.

A family of two girls and a boy are orphaned. The brother has to care for his sisters. With no money or prospects on their small hill farm, he sells his eldest sister to a trafficker. The girl is taken to a brothel in India where she is forced to work in the sex industry. The girl becomes pregnant and the brothel try and force her to have an abortion, but she pleads to be allowed to return home and have the child. Uncharacteristically they let her go, perhaps knowing she has a sister who can replace her.

I ask wasn't the girl aware of that and Probalta says that she thought her sister would be considered too young to be a prostitute and they would take another girl. But of course it is her brother who has received the money, so it is to him that the traffickers return demanding a replacement. The brother has to offer them the younger girl and she is returned with the traffickers, not realising fully where she is being sent. She too is forced to work in the brothel, and then a man offers to marry her and arrange her escape. But the younger sister has been duped for a second time, because he has arranged her escape only to make a profit out of her himself, and he sells her on to another brothel. The girl eventually does manage to escape and is now being assisted by an NGO working in this field to rebuild her life. This is the girl Probalata has interviewed.

As many young girls sold into the sex industry only escape when they have contracted AIDS, we decide to incorporate this into the story. We need to make the point that trafficking represents an early death sentence for many of its victims.

The important thing now is to stop the pupils creating comic book villains or turning the story into a melodrama. Arniko, improvising the role of the brother, is ready to embrace the Bollywood villain stereotype but I stop him. I tell him that if this story does not impact with some force and sincerity on the audience then we will have failed to get the message across. We can only do this by making the characters believable and understanding their motivations.

We discuss the brother's feelings. Why would he have done what he did? We consider the burden of having to shoulder responsibility for two female siblings, the grinding poverty, the impossibility of eking out a living working a farm without adult help, the feeling of being trapped without the possibility of escape from this grinding poverty, and of course the simple fact of the low status of girls and women in Nepal. This alone explains why traffickers, posing as potential husbands, prepared to marry girls without dowries, have been so successful. Dr Renu has sited the case of a man who 'married' 72 times and sold all his 'wives' to brothels.

We also talk about his relationship with his older sister. Having seen evidence of the tension between Arniko and Probalata who is playing the role of the oldest sister I decide to exploit it. Let's assume, I say, that you two do not get on. She tries to boss you around and as the man of the house, you think she should recognise your authority and needs taking down a peg or two. She is unlikely to get any marriage offers, in your opinion, because she is bossy and you have no dowry to offer. However, if you sell her, not only will you be able to make improvements in the farm, it will also provide you with a means of supporting your younger sister of whom you are very fond.

So why does he give the younger sister away? We discuss. Maybe he has no choice, suggests Arniko. Maybe the traffickers threaten his life if he does not hand her over.

The group try again. Rani drops in to the rehearsal and immediately the two girls playing the prostitutes become very self-conscious, which is hardly surprising, performing such an embarrassing scene in front of their Principal.

They mutter inaudibly into the ground. Sang Kalpa (playing the younger sister) under their influence also becomes self-conscious, and walks jauntily off the stage with a small smile on her face. I tell them to stop and invite responses from the audience. Galaxy, a girl from the other group who has a strong personality and a lot of potential talent, is almost bursting to offer advice. I can see that she wants to demonstrate how it should be played.

Rani intervenes with many comments I was about to make. I follow this up. I explain that the scene must be believable, but my heart sinks. I know it will take much longer than I have got to turn these girls into actors – indeed they may never develop the facility to involve themselves in parts so far from their own experience. Re-casting is essential. This is a critical moment in the story. There is a tension between the need to raise awareness, while producing a piece of theatre with impact and meaning, to a tight deadline, which can influence a wider group. I have to hope that the message will be conveyed by those with the capability to make the characters come to life, and that the momentum of working towards a performance will provide the motivation we need for the others. I feel intuitively that this approach offers the most chance of instilling an emotional understanding of the issues.

I tackle Sang Kalpa and tell her to think about the fact that she is a young, naive village girl who knows nothing about life or men, and is imbued with the moral shamefulness of sex before marriage. I explain she has just walked off the stage to be brutally deflowered as if she were just off for a nice game of tennis.

We then discuss the mechanics of how the brother could persuade the younger sister to go with the traffickers. Arniko comes up with a credible cover story that involves her deception. 'But the older sister has returned pregnant,' I say. 'She never sees the other sister,' says Arniko. I tell him he must work through the logistics with the others.

I leave them to get on with that and we review what is happening with the rag picker story. There are four young people from CWIN in this group. Two of the three lads have worked as rag pickers and all three have experienced life on the street. They are also strong actors so, understandably, this story has considerably greater impact. The Shuvatara children in this group also seem more mature so the story really works. They have taken Raj's story and have worked it through with only a few embellishments.

Haushala makes a fierce stepmother, the retiring Jyanti a believably subdued first wife. The rag pickers play themselves. Haushala reappears as a gang leader with another lad to rob the two sleeping boys of their money, but the ending is weak. Shirjit, Arniko's friend, has decided to limit his involvement to playing a comic drunk, staggering on at the end with an empty bottle and collapsing next to the two boys who have been beaten by the police. It needs a different ending.

There also needs to be some re-casting in this story. At the moment, one of the strongest girl actors is playing only a tiny part as a police officer, together with another very small girl. We discuss whether women police officers would work in pairs like that and could beat up two lads? They agree that although there are women police officers, (I have taken street directions from some), at least one of the parts needs to be taken by a male and preferably someone who is larger than the lads they are chasing. Shirjit has just got himself a second role.

We then go through the story slowly and systematically, pausing at credibility gaps and tightening up the situations. I am delighted to see that, after half an hour, we have a tight and effective story which I know will stage well, apart that is, from the ending. We even get to the point of discussing props and costumes and I am delighted to hear that CWIN (which has its own drama group) can provide some of these. I think with a bit of judicious recasting we have one story that works. Praise be.

We then break to meet up with the musicians. Only Abishek and Sodhan have brought their instruments. They have been working on the opening song and play me a quiet, reflective guitar chorus, which does not really fit the mood of the piece, although it is pleasant enough. But the verses, by contrast, are dirge-like and monotonic. I explain we need to make an impact with the opening song and ask the other musicians to get involved and to seek help from their music teachers. I tell them to adapt the words if they don't fit or create their own, as long as the theme is sustained.

The individual songs do not seem to have progressed. Arniko has been trying to fit his lyrics to an existing pop song. I explain that this is an infringement of copyright. I talk to Abishek about the mood that needs to be conveyed in the domestics' frantic 'I never stop' song. The brick workers' lyricist does not show at all.

The rag pickers, however, already have a song prepared. It's traditional, catchy, you can clap along to it. Suddenly I see how their play can end. All the cast come on dressed as street children carrying firewood. One after another they pile it in the centre of the stage to make a fire. As they sing and warm their hands, little Kusum from CWIN, who has aspirations to be a dancer, can slowly get to her feet and dance around the group.

I suggest they incorporate a final line, 'I may be poor but I am free,' because what seems to distinguishes these children from the other stories we are telling is that, despite the hazards to their health and those that come from living on the street, rag pickers have the freedom to work when they like and eat and sleep when they like. Those who end up scavenging on the dumps are often there as an escape from long exploitative hours or harsh treatment working for others. We will finish on their upbeat note, which we need as the stories that follow are much darker pieces. We should end with the domestics' story, which brings the issues close to home.

I suggest to Sunil that as an experiment, we spend some time in the afternoon trying out some Forum theatre techniques, namely that the children working on the on the brick workers' story provide the audience for the group telling the domestics' story. I suggest that we take as a scenario the young domestic summoning up her courage to ask if she can go to a 2-hour morning school for working children, like the one run by UCEP, and the family refusing because it is their busiest time of day.

We then ask the audience for suggestions as to what she should do and to act out the likely outcomes. There are four:-

'She should run away.' The group get into a huddle with Sunil and the girl acts out being picked up by a trafficker – they often prey on disgruntled or overworked domestics and carpet workers.
'She should go back to her parents.' The response is, 'but they need her to work. If she goes home they will not have enough to eat.'
'She should study at night.' The girl enacts falling asleep over a book at midnight having been up working since 5am.
'She should do nothing.' The girl becomes withdrawn, unhappy and an unwilling worker.

I then suggest a scenario where the girl from the rich family is encouraged to consolidate her own learning by teaching the domestic. My reading suggests that this sometimes happens and may be the nearest thing a domestic gets to an education. This seems to offer a compromise ending we might build on.

Sunil and I consider the effects of introducing forum theatre at the end of the play but conclude that this will not work for a number of reasons, the inexperience of the actors and the physical distance between audience and performers being just two of them. As a compromise we resolve that the children act out their suggestions and link them to a narration which ends by asking the audience, 'What would YOU do?'

Progress has been slow with the brick workers' group. We need to look carefully at how we stage this story. The research has given us little to hang a story on. I have been struck by the possibility of making this a story about a whole family, based on a case study I came across at the CWIN offices. Whole families can be trapped into virtual bonded labour because the father's quota is so high that his wife and children have to work alongside him in an attempt to fulfil it. This also makes the point that some of the children's labour may not be counted in official statistics.

I take the fragments of material home and start the long process of trying to compile them into a narrative. The play can only be part scripted. Most will be based on the children's improvisations so they keep ownership of the dialogue and action and to give the whole thing an immediacy and naturalness which I hope will add to its authenticity. I don't want to 'westernise' the play. I know everything I write will need Sunil as a touchstone to ensure authenticity of dialogue and situation.

Since the play will be acted in Nepali the simplest way to make it bi-lingual is to include an English narrator to set each scene. We can include facts and figures at the end of each story.

Rag Picker's story

Narrator: *This is Rajan's story. He was only a small child when his father took a second wife and brought her to live with Rajan and his mother. The step-mother had two daughters. The father began to beat Rajan's mother. When Rajan tried to intervene he beat him too. Finally it was too much for his mother.*

Improvised scene between Rajan and his mother outside the house. Rajan tells his mother not to cry because it makes him want to cry too. His father comes in drunk and starts to knock Rajan's mother about. Rajan tries to intervene and is hit too. We see Rajan asleep. His mother comes in with bundle. She bends down and looks at her sleeping son and then leaves.

Narrator: *With his mother gone, Rajan was left to the mercy of his step-mother.*

Scene 2

Step-mother and her daughters ill-treat Rajan. The father takes the step-mother's part. Rajan runs away.

Narrator: *Rajan was only seven when he left home, penniless. It took him weeks to reach Kathmandu where he dreamed of getting a job in a hotel. He was successful, if you can call working a 16 hour day and sleeping in a corridor successful.*

Scene Three: The hotel

Rajan is scrubbing the floor. Another worker comes up and talks to him, they find they are from the same district. She says she is running away and warns him that the hotel cheats by not paying you at the end of the month.

Narrator: *The worker warned Rajan the hotel would not pay him for his work and said she was going to run away. So Rajan ran away too. What kind of life would he find on the street? Would it be like this?*

Screening of 'Life on the Street'

Scene Four: The junk yard

The rag pickers come down into the audience and collect litter in their sack. The junk-yard owner (on stage) gestures them to exit left and get their load weighed. They return and hand him a slip; he hands them a few notes. They protest he has short-changed them. He tells them to go – they are ignorant and cannot add up – who are they to question him?

Narrator: *The scrap yard owner accused the boys of being ignorant when they said he had given them too little money. (Aside to the audience) Of course he cheated them. What will they do now? Eat tonight or go hungry till tomorrow?*

Scene 5: On the streets

The rag pickers settle down to sleep on pieces of cardboard with their sacks. They are hungry but decide to eat in the morning. They decide to hide the money under the cardboard in case they are robbed.

Gang members enter. Bikash wakes with a start as they approach. He tries to wake Rajan, gives up and runs away. The gang attack Rajan, pull him up and go through his pockets – kick the cardboard in disgust when they find nothing and uncover the money. They run off. Rajan screams after them – his mate returns – they argue, but decide that there is no point getting angry with each other because the gang were bigger than them anyway. They decide to steal some food.

A banana seller comes on. One boy agrees to distract her while the other pinches the bananas. A child (Kusum) comes on and sees them. She calls her mother who comes out and shouts for the police. Two police run on and pursue the rag pickers into the audience (the boys throw the bananas to someone in the auditorium). The police chase them round the auditorium and back onto the stage. They beat the two boys, search them for money, and exit. The rag pickers slump to the ground.

Gradually, one by one, other rag pickers come on stage carrying firewood and put their sticks down in a central bundle to make a fire. They sit around the fire in a half circle – Shirjit comes in with bottle of alcohol in his hand and slumps to the ground. Gradually they begin singing the rag pickers' song. Kusum gets up and dances. Raju shouts, *'I may be poor but I am free!'*

We will need some back projection after each story to reinforce the message.

Rivers of Shame
4,000 children are estimated to rag pick in urban Nepal
They collect glass, plastic, rags and metal
from dumps and river banks

Rivers of Shame
They are exposed to: Cuts, abrasions, sores and
animal bites and stomach upsets from eating contaminated food
27,000 children die from diarrhoea every year in Nepal

Rivers of Shame
They are vulnerable to assault, rape, theft, drugs and crime,
tetanus and other blood-borne diseases
HIV and AIDS

Thursday April 18th

The heat in the hall is oppressive, despite the massive overhead fans. I realise that if we are to make progress I will have to continue compiling the scripts on my own, albeit with Sunil's advice. I suggest retiring after lunch to start doing so, as I am taking a weekend break in Chitwan.

I am feeling restless and cooped up, desperate for a change of scene. I am only too aware how much there is to see in this fascinating country and how little time there is to see it all. One part of me thinks I should not leave Sunil because of his diffidence with the Shuvatara children. Gifted and as experienced as he is, he does not seem able or willing to exert any discipline over them.

He gets on better with the young people from CWIN. They have been toughened through adversity, are focused, and serious about a subject that is close to them. Life has made them mature early – as it has Sunil. It is magic to see them open up and begin to enjoy themselves because joy is something that has been singularly lacking in so much of their lives. The boys act convincingly and with authority, although the girls, starved of love and affection, need a huge amount of confidence boosting. I am not sure either of us is equipped to provide them with what they need, although Sunil has insights it would take me a life-time to acquire.

Despite this, I also find it easier and more rewarding to watch the CWIN kids. While I am quite fond of some of the school children, some are difficult and I wonder how much of this is really sinking in and making an impression on them. Rani is defensive of her privileged children and feels the CWIN kids benefit from 'knowing that people care.' Some do care, but the vast majority? I think the message is just not getting through and that bothers me, because isn't the process of this experiment more important than the product?

I have become increasingly aware as my departure looms that I am not looking forward to leaving. Back home all I seem to face is endings, whereas in Nepal it has been a series of beginnings. I still wrestle to maintain emotional equilibrium. Working with such powerful and disturbing themes seems to accord with this inner turmoil.

I have to be careful to control my emotions and redirect them into this work in a productive way. I think we should be angry about things that are patently cruel and unjust and the issue of child labour cries out for that kind of passionate response. I know it is a quality in me that makes Rani uneasy. It is our fundamental difference. But part of rediscovering who I am, is to try and channel my own passion in order to teach these young people to care, through my writing, my teaching or both.

I will also have to be unpopular. Some recasting is needed now we are more aware of what the children can do. I phone Galaxy and tell her I want her in the girls' trafficking story because she has a strong voice and stage presence. She is enthusiastic but troubled that she cannot attend on Friday. I don't mind too much. I sense she will be very committed and that the story will benefit considerably from this recasting.

There are many issues in the girls' trafficking story that I worry about. How we can deal with them all instead of just telling one girl's horror story? I don't want to demonise any one character because the fundamental problem lies not with the individual but with the patriarchal society in which the life of a girl counts for so little.

Despite the fact that the government of Nepal has prepared a five-year plan – ostensibly dealing with the problems of gender exploitation by providing legal redress, medical help, education, training and income generating programmes for the survivors of trafficking - there is widespread consensus that these programmes and plans are, at best, very superficial or simply limited to paper. The present development model still upholds the patriarchal norms. These are entrenched in Nepal's laws, that deny women paternal property rights. Illegitimate children are denied citizenship, which restricts their access to education and other rights. Many women still need to get married to survive. If their husbands abuse them they have no resources or places to go.

Selective abortions of female foetuses are known to occur through much of South East Asia. The Regional Health Report for 1998 produced by the World Health Organisation found in one study of an urban area that, out of 8,000 abortions performed after the parents had learned the sex of the foetus, only one was male. Abortion is illegal in Nepal[2] – which does not mean it isn't performed – but there are other ways in which the surviving girl child is discriminated against. Under-fives mortality rates

2. No longer the case. See footnote page 61

are higher among girls because of malnutrition and neglect. This, in turn, leads to impaired intellectual development, delayed puberty and stunted growth. These factors, coupled with the tradition of early marriage, mean the girls are often not fully developed physically or mentally, and complications during childbirth are frequent. I start the girls' story with all these thoughts buzzing around my head.

Girls' Trafficking story

Narrator: *This is a story of three orphaned children, two sisters and a brother, trying to make a living on a small hill farm. In desperate poverty, the brother sells his elder sister, Maya, to a trafficker in order to survive. She disappears to an Indian brothel. Now she has returned, pregnant, but the price of her freedom is that she must be replaced.*
The brothel has sent two people to ensure this happens.....

Scene One:

Maya returns home pregnant. Her brother is furious. She tells him that she has fought against an abortion and for the right to return home to have her child, but the brothel are sending two people after her determined they will be given a replacement. She says she is desperate and could think of nothing to do but come home. He tells her to get out, that he does not want her younger sister to see her like that. She has brought shame on the family.

A trafficker (Pukar) and prostitute (Galaxy) arrive and threaten the brother, 'You have had our money, so find us a replacement. Don't you have a younger sister?' He tries to resist, 'But she is so young.' They threaten to kill him. He calls in his younger sister (Sang Kalpa). He tells her he has heard her other sister has run away from her job and that these people have come to take her as a replacement. The visitors make a fuss of the girl and tell her she will have a nice job. Although hesitant, she goes off willingly, not knowing she is being sent to a brothel. As an after-thought they tell her that to avoid trouble with the police she is to pretend Pukar is her husband and Galaxy her sister-in-law. She laughs at the idea.

Maya (Probalta) enters, distraught that her sister is the one taken, and collapses in tears. Her brother tells her she is to blame

Narrator: *So Kanchi, the youngest sister, was taken to India in her sister's place, not knowing where she was being taken.*

Scene Two: In the brothel

Galaxy enters with the girl. The brothel Madam (Ganga) asks Kanchi to turn round so she can look at her and then asks her to sit down. Galaxy exits. The girl asks where she is and what she is to do. The Madam tells her this is a sort of hotel. Kanchi asks if she will be cleaning. 'No,' she is told, 'we are going to give you an easier job than that.' 'Will I make the beds?' asks Kanchi – 'well, you will be doing some work in the bedroom,' says the Madam with a smirk. 'What will I have to do?' asks Kanchi. The brothel owner tells her that she needs hostesses who are pretty because they get a lot of customers who are lonely men and who want some company. All she will have to do is to wear pretty clothes like a film star and be obliging. 'That's not so hard, is it?' Kanchi looks confused and says nothing. 'Let me look at your hands,' says the Madam. She takes Kanchi's hands and examines them. 'Hmm, just as I thought, all rough and dirty. We must make you a bit more beautiful.' She rings a small bell at her side. Two young prostitutes enter and eye up the new recruit. One applies make-up to the girl while the other takes off her head-scarf and starts combing her hair. Galaxy comes in wearing a dressing gown with a customer (Shirjit). Kanchi stares open-mouthed at her. The prostitute who is making her up yanks her head back. They fit bangles on her arms and beads round her neck.

They take her behind a screen and she comes out decked in a gaudy top and a mini skirt. She walks awkwardly on high-heeled shoes. She stands there uncertainly. One prostitute holds out her hand and says, 'Come along and meet one of our customers.' The girl becomes uneasy. She looks down at her short skirt and begins to back towards the screen. The prostitute grabs her hand and pulls her roughly downstage saying, 'Come on now, don't get difficult after all the trouble we have gone to.' Kanchi is dragged offstage. As the other prostitute starts to gather up the make-up we hear

Kanchi shouting off stage 'No no NO,' pause, and then a scream.

Narrator: Kanchi was kept in the brothel for nine months and forced to have sex with up to ten men a night. If she refused she was locked up, kept without food and beaten. Once she thought she had been rescued when a regular customer told her he wanted to marry her. He arranged her escape, but it was another cruel deception. He sold Kanchi on to another brothel for 25,000 rupees.
(Music: Kanchi comes on and slumps on a chair)

Narrator: *Kanchi fell ill. She lost weight and became very pale. After some months strange red lesions began to break out on her skin. Her illness was to be the means of her escape when a customer suspected what was wrong.*

A customer comes in and asks what is wrong. He takes Kanchi's hand and rubs her arm, which pushes up her sleeve. He sees the marks and freezes. 'Have you got any more of these?' he asks. He pushes her forward like a rag doll and looks on her neck. She has them here too. He pulls her up and drags her to the door. The brothel keeper is there. He asks, 'Don't you know this girl is sick?' The brothel keeper shrugs. The man gets angry, 'Don't you know she may have AIDS? If I have caught anything here you will be sorry,' he says raising his fist. The brothel owner backs away. 'AIDS!' she shrieks. 'Take her. She is no use to me if she has AIDS.' Kanchi staggers. 'Come on,' says the man, 'I need to know if I am right'.

Narrator: *A doctor confirmed the worst. Kanchi had contracted HIV and AIDS. Eventually, with help from various agencies she was returned home. Her sister's joy on seeing Kanchi was short-lived. She had to come to terms with the fact that the price of her child's life was her sister's death.*

Scene 3: In the hills

Maya comes on holding a baby. She sees her sister and runs forward overjoyed. Kanchi collapses. 'What's wrong?' says Maya. 'I am going to die,' says her sister. Maya is stunned. 'Why? Why?' she asks, and Kanchi tells her. Maya is dazed – she looks down at her baby. 'Have I done that to you?' she asks. She picks up the child and turns towards the audience. 'Is the price of my child's life, my sister's death?'

Gradually, other villagers join them. One woman tries to comfort Maya. 'We must never let what has happened to you and your sister happen here again,' says the woman. 'Men and women should be able to leave to find work without the risk of losing their lives or being enslaved. We will organise to stop this.' 'Yes, and if we got together and organised our farms better we could help each other through our hardships,' says an old man.

The brother comes on and freezes when he sees the group. They turn and point threateningly towards him.

Narrator: *The villagers decide they will not let this happen again. They must organise to stop trafficking. Women and men should be free to leave to find work but not to be sold. They vow to try and find ways to help each other through their hardships.* **ENDS**

Rivers Of Shame
Girls' trafficking: Global Statistics
Up to 2 million people, mainly women and children, are being trafficked annually. Human trafficking is the 3rd biggest illegal trade after drugs smuggling and gun running netting $5-$7 billion annually.

Rivers Of Shame
Girls' trafficking: Global Statistics
The present rate of trafficking in children is already TEN TIMES higher than the TRANSATLANTIC SLAVE TRADE at its peak.

The next story caused me some problems. The research we had picked up from the children was very sparse or too similar to other stories. This is what we had:

Visit to San Goan site - outskirts of Kathmandu.

The site produces bricks for six months and cultivates rice in the fields the other six months. Anju has been told by the owner the site produces 1,200 bricks per day, yet I have read accounts of this amount being churned out by just one or two workers. On our second brick site visit, when I tell Anju to check the individual output, the bus driver tells her that she should never ask the manager for confirmation. 'He will never tell you the real figures,' he says. 'If he did so, the government would demand more tax.'

There are three processes at the site: digging out the raw clay and making trenches for water collection, moulding and drying the bricks, and firing the bricks. Nepalis are rarely used in the firing process as they cannot withstand the heat as well as workers from India and the Terai. The latter have the hardest, and, marginally, best paid work.

Most of the people on the site are family groups. The Nepalese families come mainly from the rural West of Nepal, Rolpa, Dang, and Rukkum. There are 50-55 families on the site, 40 working around the chimneys. All the children, starting at age three or four, work, carrying bricks or moulding them. How much they carry depends on their size rather than their age. Some children come to work without their families. The majority have no education. The average number of bricks a labourer carries on his head is twelve, women carry up to 36 on a harness down their back. Every time a labourer transports a load he is given a rubber token. At the end of the day the tokens are exchanged for wages. On average they get 80 rupees a day (70p).

I decided to concentrate on the children of working families whose labour, I was pretty sure, goes unrecorded, meaning that there is a vast under-representation of children working in the industry. With 55 families on site and no birth control, even allowing for high infant mortality, that probably means an average of four children per family. That's 220 children in one SMALL brickworks. Multiply that by the 179 brickyards we know of in the Kathmandu valley alone, and it gives you a figure of 35,300. Even if the figures are halved, it makes the Ministry of Labour total of fewer than 2,000 child brick workers look absurd.

Some fathers bring their children reluctantly to the sites but are in a near bonded situation and have little choice. I have read one such moving case. By looking at a family who care about their children, I can also make the point that working children are not just a product of 'wicked stepmothers'. It is so easy to demonise one section of the population and claim they are responsible for child labour when it is more to do with grinding poverty.
I look at the pupils' research. This is what we have: I have deleted the names.

Brick worker profiles
Bhaktapur Factory

PG (15): has been at the factory for two years. His mother died when he was very young. His father remarried when he was seven. His stepmother forced him onto a bus to another village where he survived doing chores. He has received no education. He hardly remembers his father. He works from 3am to 7pm and gets 6000 rupees after six months – about 250rupees per week. He is still receives no education and has no plans or expectations.

SN (14): was brought here by her brother from Rolpa when she was 12. She carries 28 bricks at a time and says raw bricks are not too heavy. Her family consists of parents, five elder brothers and their wives – her eldest brother has two wives, and two younger sisters. She was sent to work here because of poverty. She earns 6-9000 rupees every six months. She has received education to Class 2 and would like to study further. She complains of leg, back and body pain, especially at night, and suffers from nightmares. She is unhappy and wants to go home, but at least here she has enough to eat.

PN (15): Also from Rolpa. His brother brought him to work here two years ago. He has two older brothers and one older sister, and still has contact with his family. He earns 5-6000 rupees every 6 months – less than 35 rupees a day. He suffers leg and back pain. He has had an education to Class 3. He has no thoughts for the future.

AKP (15): from Dumja, has four brothers and sisters and parents who farm. He was sent here three years ago due to poverty, and is with his brother-in-law. He has had an education to Class 3 and works moulding and carrying bricks from 6am-6pm earning about 4,450 rupees every six months. He has had no contact with his family since he left home but sends then all his money. He suffers from back and stomach pains for which he receives no medical help. He would like to become someone great and rescue his family from poverty

PG (12): is from Dang in the Terai. Six years ago, unable to support the family from his farming, his father sent him to the site. PG is now responsible for supporting his parents and two younger brothers. He has received no education and is envious of those that have. He works from 4am to 6pm, carrying ten bricks at a time on his back and is paid 3,000 rupees per month, depending on how much work he has done. He suffers neck and back pain, breathing problems and nightmares. He is often depressed, anxious and cannot sleep. He receives no medical attention. His dearest wish is an education. The adult workers bully him.

K (13): also from Dang, in the Terai, has been coming to the brick site for two years. His mother died in childbirth when he was six. His father died of alcohol-related illnesses. His uncle took care of his younger sisters but could not afford to take care of K, so he was sent to a brick factory to help reduce their hardship. A few years ago, when he returned to his village, he found his uncle had died, his eldest sister had been sold to a brothel in India and his two younger sisters were working in the village as domestics. He brought them to the brickyards to work with him as he did not want to take the risk of them getting sold as well. All three of them are still there. He dreams of meeting his eldest sister one day.

PG (15): from Dhangadi, has been working on the site for a year. His mother died when he was very young. His father took a new wife when he was seven, but his stepmother forced him on to a bus and sent him away to another village. He has received no education and hardly remembers his father. He survived doing odd jobs in the neighbouring village and now works at the brick works from 3am to 7pm and gets Rs 6,000 (roughly £60) for 6 months work. He gets 2 meals a day. He has had no education and has no future plans. At the moment his health is good. He considers he is treated well at the brickyards.

N (11): first came to the site with his family, when he was six, and has been coming ever since. He has received no education, starts work at 6am and finishes at 3pm. He makes 200 bricks a day and carries 6-8 bricks at a time. He suffers back pains, and aches in his head and shoulders. Each member of the family gets 200 rupees a week.

N (15): was sent here to work with his two brothers when his parents fell into debt. His hours are 3am to 7pm with couple of hours' lunch break. He and his younger brother make 1,500 to 1,600 bricks a day between them and carry up to 12 bricks at a time. N used to study at home in Ramechap and got to Grade 5 but now receives no education. His wage is 250 rupees a week. All his wages are given to his parents.

MN (15): is here with her mother, elder brother and sister. She comes from a remote part of Rolpa. Her family have had to leave their home in the care of a neighbour to search for work. Her father is in India. She has never been educated as there is no school near her home. She carries bricks.

These accounts are typical of hundreds of similar stories of extreme poverty, deprivation and exploitation but I need more than the bare facts.

I begin to weave a story around a case study CWIN has published about a 35-year-old farmer from Dhulikhel who came to work at a brick site in Patan. He had to bring his family to the site because the quota of bricks he was expected to produce was beyond his capabilities and the recruiters held his property papers as security against an advanced loan he had been unable to repay. His heath had deteriorated and so had that of all his children. His wife said the site was like a desert – it's how I felt too. I was struck by something the father said: 'They take every single thing you call your own.' I give him the name Nima and call his son Dil.

Brick Maker's story

Narrator: *This is a story of Nima Tamang, a poor farmer from Rolpa. He has two daughters, one son and another child on the way. He is about to make a decision to work in the brick sites which will affect his whole family.*

A recruiter contracts Nima to mould 100,000 bricks in a six-month season. His wage? 100 rupees for every 1,200 bricks – the expected daily rate – minus 10% he must give to the recruiter. In return he gets a loan of 2,500 rupees to keep his family while he is away, but he must surrender his citizenship and property papers as security for the loan. He seals the deal with his thumb. He never learned to write.

Scene1: The hill village

A naike (recruiter) visits the village and strikes a contract with Nima – a loan of 2,500 rupees in exchange for the production of 100,000 bricks over six months. The naike very deliberately counts out the money. Nima signs the agreement with his thumb, telling his youngest child to fetch the property papers from the house.

His wife comes in with the papers and wants to know why he wants the documents. She is dismayed he is going away for six months with their baby due, but he reminds her they will soon have another mouth to feed. The naike points to the father's pocket to indicate he has been paid.

The children enter, tired from their long walk back from school. The father tells them they must forget about school now – they are 10 and 11 – old enough to help their mother run the farm while he is away. The son says he will help, but the daughter is unhappy about giving up school. The father says her mother cannot manage alone – anyway why does a girl need an education? She will only grow up to be a burden, 'it's like throwing a coin in a river.' He promises to be back in six months – he is strong – he is sure he can fulfil the quota.

Back projection of a brick site

Narrator: *So Nima came to the brick site. He thought he would manage to make up his quota working a 16 hour day but it wasn't so easy. He fell ill, ate poorly and developed breathing problems – and then there was the unseasonable rain...*

Scene 2: The brick site

(Thunder at night. Darkened stage lightening illuminates rows of bricks. Workers run on from both sides as the sound of rain is heard and start to load up the bricks and carry them off.)

Overseer: *(with umbrella directs operation)* Quick, quick, try and get some of them under cover or the week's quota will be ruined. *(All freeze. Thunder. Nima comes downstage and addresses the audience)*

Nima: We lost many bricks that season due to rain. I had to return home in debt and without my papers. I had no choice. Next season I had to bring the whole family back to help me. *(Exits. Workers unfreeze and back off stage)*

Narrator: *Nima returned home without his papers and even deeper in debt – on top of the original loan was money he had to borrow to feed himself. He had no choice but to return with his family the following season.*

(*Light goes up on the stage*)

Mother: *(upstage right comes on carrying a bucket – looks around)* It's like a desert here.

Daughter: *(enter downstage left. She is unrecognisably dirty and is carrying a stack of bricks on her back, she sees her mother with the bucket, unhitches her bricks and comes and takes the bucket)*

I'll take this to the water tap – you have both father and the baby, sick .

(Mother goes out the way she came. Dill and Ram come on wearing dirty vests – they are both carrying 10 fired bricks on their head).

Dil: *(seeing his sister turning to go upstage)* Hey, where are you going with that bucket?

Daughter: I'm getting water at the tap.

Dil: There is no time for that; you need to get all the bricks moved.

Ram: Anyway what's the point of going all the way to the tap?

Sister: Who is this boy?

Ram: My name is Ram

Dil: He is showing me how to carry bigger loads. He's been coming here alone since he was seven – he earns 60 rupees a day.

Sister: Well, you must earn for the family.

Ram: But I earn for my family in the Terai too. I must take money home each season. I work on the kilns too – you can earn more money there, though it's only Indians and the Terai folk who can take the heat, not like you people from the hills.

Sister: Well, I must get the water.

Dil: No! *(Puts bricks down)* Give me the bucket!

(He goes down stage and lowers the bucket over the side of the stage. Mother comes on with Sita the younger girl who has the baby tied on her back. She frowns when she sees what Dil is doing- she bends down with Sita and mimes to her that she must mould bricks. The older girl looks over the edge of the stage)

Sister: Should we use the water from the clay pit?

Ram: Well, I do – all of us do – the water tap is too far away and anyway the water only comes out in a dribble.

(Mother gets up and starts to walk over to them. Dil hands the bucket to girl)

Girl: *(looks in the bucket)* At home we get water from the stream.

Ram: Well you are not at home now. I hope my sister won't make a fuss when she arrives.

Sister: You have a sister?

Ram: Yes, she is coming here because the inspectors have told her she can't stay in the carpet factory. They say it's against the law and not healthy for children. [3]

Mother: *(takes the bucket and looks in it)* And this is healthy? *(She frowns)*

Ram: Well it's a job and no one inspects us here – she has to work. We

3. I mentioned Rugmark in the first version but the ILO asked me to remove the reference because they are supposed to help displaced child labourers find alternatives which are better, not worse.

don't make enough on the farm to feed us all for more than three months of the year. What else is there?
(Mother frowns and thoughtfully carries off bucket upstage right)
Dil: We must get on. (*They pick up their bricks)*
Ram: *(looks at girl and grins)* Bet you can't do this! *(he balances on one leg with the bricks on his head).*
Overseer: *(comes in with a stick – to Ram)* What are you doing? *(Ram hastily puts his foot down.)*
Overseer: *(raises his stick – Ram flinches)* I don't pay you to play – get back to work – or else… you know what this stick feels like, don't you? *(Overseer wheels round to Dill)* And where is your father?
Dil: *(nervously)* He is sick – but he will be better soon – we can manage.
Overseer: Well, you and your sister had better look to it or you'll feel my stick too – your quota is slipping!
Girl: *(lifts bricks and exits upstage right. As she passes her sister she says)* Sita, you must make the bricks on your own, I have to help Dil.

Narrator: *Two months pass. Nima's son developed a skin disease and terrible back pains, one of his daughter's an infected sore on her eye that would not heal. They have food here but little appetite.*
(Blackout: during the narration the family come on in and lie down to sleep in a huddle - son next to mother – Dil moans in his sleep and cries out in pain – father rolls over restlessly)
Mother: What is it? Must you disturb your father? He must sleep. He has to be at work again at 3 this morning.
Dil: I can't help it, my neck and back hurt so.
Mother: Come outside with me and walk around for a bit till you can straighten up.
(Dil rolls over, gets up painfully stooping and limps off stage with mother. The others roll up bedding and exit in blackout during narration.)

Narrator: *Children carrying loads too heavy for them before their spines have finished growing, can end up with spinal deformities. Women carrying 36 bricks strapped to their back all day can suffer cervical prolapses, especially when they are back at work within days of giving birth.*

Next scene

(Daughter comes on upstage left with brick mould. She bends down to mould bricks. Noise of baby crying off stage).

Mother: *(runs on with hands over her ears)* Stop it! Stop it! Stop it! I can't stand it! He won't suckle now – he pushes me away – he is skin and bone. What have we done? What have we done?

(She collapses crying, daughter drops brick mould and comes to comfort mother. Suddenly the crying stops. Mother listens tensely NO! she runs off stage followed by daughter)

Final scene

(Father comes in leading a procession with rest of family and carrying a small bundle in a winding sheet. He lays it on the ground centre downstage. Nepali musicians sing a song of mourning)[4]

Narrator: *A tiny life lost. They came here to work or die of hunger – is this the best we can do for our children?*

Father: They take from you every single thing you call your own. **END**

Rivers Of Shame

1998 Minister of Labour figures estimated nearly 2,000 child brick workers working the brick kilns of the Kathmandu valley alone. The figures are a vast underestimation. The industry has been growing rapidly since then.

Rivers Of Shame

Children as young as six carry heavy weights which increase with their age and size. Respiratory illness and spinal deformities are common.

Rivers Of Shame

Children come with poor families who are bonded labour on their own, or through a recruiter...

4. *The Nepali music teacher devised a very moving traditional song only two days before the production*

...The wage of 100 rupees a day
for the production of 1,200 bricks is not uncommon.
Bricks spoilt by rain mean lost income for the workers.

The final story I tackle is about Domestic Service. We should finish with this story because it offers an opportunity to ask the audience what they are going to do about the problem. I have arranged for a number of NGOs to have exhibitions in the foyer of the theatre so there are opportunities for people to get involved straight away if they chose to do so. Striking while the iron is hot.

There are 55,000 child domestics in Nepal, 22,000 in Kathmandu alone. One in five families employs a child domestic. That means Shuvatara children's parents employ a fair number, which brings the story close to home. I am going to have to be careful with this one if I want to keep the integrity of the story without alienating the children or their parents. I have to presume their parents are fair employers, but the invisibility and lack of representation of many of these children allows opportunities for gross mistreatment and exploitation. I have already seen enough at one small brick site, owned by a parent, to know such an assumption may be over-optimistic.

Either way I feel we should discount 'research' which involves the students asking their own domestic if she feels exploited. One girl actually did this and came back with the answer that child's future wish was 'to be good and work hard'. To paraphrase Mandy Rice-Davis, 'she would say that, wouldn't she?'

Some of the CWIN children have been domestics. Their stories suggest other, less benign, realities. Superficially it is not difficult in such a poor country to understand why city life has tremendous attractions for destitute people from rural areas. Domestic service is seen as a secure position that guarantees food, clothing, shelter and, sometimes, even an education. Poor parents regard life as a kanchi (little sister) as a better life than they could provide at home. In fact, few servants see a classroom. Employers say that they or their children teach the servant at home. There is no limit to what domestic work may involve, from washing, cleaning, babysitting, cooking, gardening, to helping with the construction of a well or water tank, even acting as labourers fetching cement and clearing rubble.

Most domestics have no employment contract. They are often employed through brokers who cheat the parents as well as the children, keeping the bulk of the child's earnings. Many children work just for food and find the notion of a wage an incredible idea. They work 12 or more hours a day for just two basic meals.

Most houses don't bother with overpriced labour-saving devices like vacuum cleaners or washing machines – a servant is cheaper – so there are no aids to help with the backbreaking work. I was saddened to read of one twelve year old girl, a poor relation who loved TV but who had to sit outside the door to watch it – she was not allowed in with the family. She had to carry the children's bags to school but never went herself and had to use the honorific term for 'you' when addressing them. Yet these children were the same age as her and related by blood.

I suspect her employers, like many middle-class people I have met, are peaceful and benign on the surface but capable of ignoring exploitation when they wish to. Even Rani, who is always telling me how her husband is a model employer will tell you in the same breath how he kept a labourer working at the house until 1.30am knocking down a wall, without any sense of contradiction.

I have the sense of a society in blinkers, with a prosperous elite who avoid seeing what is under their own noses because it would inconvenience them too much to recognise it. It was, and I am sure still is, the same in South Africa and in India – call it class, call it caste – I hate it and it stinks. Being here has sharpened my political views once more. I am glad I still feel so angry about such things. To stop is to surrender to complacency.

There is much fuel for my anger. This is just one appalling account I came across. It involves a case documented by CWIN as part of campaign to release a 13-year-old boy domestic being held in an adult prison for murder of a young girl domestic worker. A judge employed both servants and the girl was murdered in his house. When he called the police, the judge explained the cause of the death as an accident, but it was later discovered the girl had been raped and suffocated and a number of corroborating witnesses pointed to the judge's son as the main culprit. Instead, the 13-year-old male domestic was accused by the judge of being the one responsible, though there was nothing to link the boy with the murder. The judge used his influence to have the boy thrown into gaol. CWIN are campaigning for his release. Nothing has happened to the judge or his son.

Another example is Indian domestic Apsana Begum. She tried to commit suicide by jumping from the window of a tall building because she was unable to bear the daily torture, beatings and false accusations of her employer Nisha Katum. She survived but was severely injured. Concerned neighbours had her admitted to hospital. It was decided that her case needed police action, but Nisha's brother in law 'negotiated' with the police to treat the case as a minor one. Rahman, her recruiter, who had also tortured her, was then contacted and given 100 rupees to return her to West Bengal, falsely accusing her of 'troubling her employers.'

However a journalist heard the story and helped the girl to report the case to the district police headquarters. CWIN also investigated the case and, as a consequence, filed a case against her employers and prosecuted Rahman for trafficking the girl from India.

I regret that it is not possible to prepare a stronger piece, but I must restrict myself to what we have researched. I also regret missing one incident out of the play, where one of the CWIN children was sacked for leaving the premises of her employers without permission to buy tea at the request of some family visitors.

Domestic's story

(Back projection - 3 slides The Child in Domestic Labour: Picture of Child: Statistics of Domestics)

Narrator: *My father and mother were loving, I was lucky there. But there was no money in our home. One day help was offered.*

Scene one

A recruiter enters. He tells the parents he can offer their daughter work in the city and suggests that she will be able to go to school. 'You would like that, wouldn't you?' *he asks the daughter. He puts her at ease by reminding her how long he has known her family. He haggles with the father about how much he should pay him for settling his daughter. The daughter is won over by the possibility of going to school.*

Daughter: Well, there is no school in my village and I want to write my name, add up, and help my parents too.

Recruiter: And you shall – I have a family in mind. They want help in their house. They are kind and will feed you and your money will be sent to your father every six months.

Daughter: And school?

Recruiter: Oh sure, there are lots of schools in Kathmandu.

Daughter: I'll go if you let me, father, mother?

Father: *(sighing)* We have no choice, but you must be good and work hard. We need your money.

Daughter: And you shall have it, and I shall have school! I'll work hard you'll see.

Daughter: *(narrating in English to audience)* I meant to work hard, but I little knew what would happen.

Scene 2: Family house in Kathmandu

The recruiter introduces the girl to the family. They run through a huge summary of duties starting at 5am, keep interrupting each other about new duties they would like her to undertake and then get increasingly vague about when she should finish. The girl looks more and more subdued and goes off with head bowed.

Girl: *(narrates)*: I worked and worked – I had to be up till the last person was in bed – and sometimes the last person, a man, behaved towards me in a way that I did not like. I was unhappy and after two months I ran away. My parents did not try to make me go back. I was found a new job;

there were children here too and they went to school.
(Stage Left – domestic in kitchen scrubs clothes . Stage Right – child upstairs yawns and reaches for Walkman<blast of house music> Stage Left 'downstairs' cleaner scrubs the floor, 'upstairs' girl reads a magazine, downstairs girl rings out clothes takes them outside and hangs them on the line, girl upstairs yawns and calls for a drink of water, domestic brings in water. Girl tells domestic to turn on the shower for her and iron her school blouse. Domestic goes out – mother wants to know when she intends to get around to breakfast – girl mimes boiling water, chopping vegetables making drinks, opening fridge – scream from upstairs 'Where is my blouse?' *Girl stops what she is doing, gets out ironing board and iron and starts ironing blouse – girl upstairs, 'Where is my blouse – are you deaf?' Domestic takes up the blouse and gets clipped on the ear. She sinks to the floor and wipes away a tear.)*

Girl: *(narrates)*: And all this time I dreamt about school, but I only got as far as the school gates when I carried the children's bags. I was scared to ask, but one day I summoned up my courage when I heard about a morning school for working children.

Next Scene: The girl asks her employers if she can go to school. The family put up lots of objections, distance – time out of the house at the most busy time of the day. No, no, quite out of the question.
Girl: *(narrates)*: I should not have asked – I knew it would be too much to expect. Now I feel I will never learn things and I am so sad, I feel as if my heart will break.

New Narrator: *What should she do? Let's think this one through. Should she run away, maybe? Let's see what happens.*
Second Narrator: *Repeats narration in Nepali*
(We see a scene where a trafficker picks up the domestic)
Narrator(s)(in English then Nepali): *Runaway girls can easily fall prey to traffickers. So that won't do. Well, her parents still love her, so home is obviously the best place. (Girl seen starting to pack a small bag)*
Narrator: *Hang on. (Girl stops packing and thinks) How will her parents*

keep her when she has been keeping them? So that won't do.
Narrator: *She could study at night (Girl shown reading but keeps falling asleep).*
Narrator: *Too weary? Oh well....*

Daughter: *(yells)* Someone help me with my revision.
Mother: You always leave everything to the last minute. Why can't you study properly? I cannot help now, I'm late for a meeting.
Daughter: But mum...
Mother: When I was your age I recited things over or tried teaching things to my little sister – that way the subject really stuck.
(She goes to exit, then is struck by a thought, she wheels round)
Why not teach the girl?
Daughter: What?
Mother: Use the girl – teach her things – you've got plenty of old exercise books. *(she looks at the girl who was dusting but is now listening carefully)* You heard me – teach her. Who knows, you might cheer her up a bit and it will help you a bit too.
(she hugs her daughter then waves her goodbye)

Narrator: So is there hope? Can something be done? Only you can decide. These were just four stories, there are thousands more, but how many do you need? Did we make them up? No, not one word, but we could have told worse – when children are treated like commodities anything can happen – ever wonder where all the organs for transplants come from?

We can't wait till tomorrow. Make the first step today.
The children of the world are waiting *(Blackout)* **END**

Back projection

Rivers Of Shame

An estimated 55,000 children under the age of 18, work as domestic servants in Nepal. 22,000 are in Kathmandu alone. Abuse, rape and confinement to employers' premises are known to occur.

Rivers Of Shame

'A child is still one more hope
Even in this careworn world… A child is still one more child
Even in arms of stone.' Shuntaro Tanikawa

Rivers Of Shame

Don't leave it till tomorrow. Get involved today
The children of the world are WAITING

The ending to the domestic's story is not very dramatic but I needed to end on a hopeful note. There is no point alienating the audience when I want to prick their conscience into some positive action.

The idea for the ending came from something I read in Mandela, the magazine of the Nepal Centre of the International Theatre Institute about Kachahari theatre – a kind of interactive theatre where the audience direct a performance about their own lives. The first part of their play is performed by actors, who have observed the conflicts in the village. They build the first part of the play to a conflict moment and then ask the audience what they should do now. As the audience comes up with suggestions the actors show them on the spot – it is an adaptation of Augusto Boal's Forum Theatre.

The role of comedy was stressed, described as 'the ability to pull the rubber band of tension with the audience' and to keep them identifying with the play. I am glad the children have incorporated many light touches in our play.

I finally finish writing at 2am and put it in an envelope for Sunil to pick up in the morning and flesh out the scenes in Nepali. I've done it! I've compiled a play. I can't claim to have exactly 'written' a play, but have at least drawn together the improvisations into what I hope will be a logical whole, incorporating our joint research along the way. I have always been an admirer of the British director Mike Leigh and hope I have emulated his rehearsal techniques at least a little.

I am reminded that Victoria Wood said her first play was written before she realised how difficult it was to write one, and David Hare's debut script was knocked out on a portable typewriter in the back of a van hurtling to some rural venue. I'm not making comparisons, far from it, except to note that maybe you have to be pushed into these things…

I reckon I've earned my weekend. I have exactly four hours to catch some sleep before setting off for Chitwan.

Friday April 19th:
In limbo in Chitwan

Early morning Kathmandu: stink of shit from the river, barbers on the side-walk solemnly shaving a group of men on a line of chairs, draped in white sheets, porters with baskets of fruit, neatly dressed school children, joggers, beggars, callisthenics in Ratna Park. On the opposite side of the park, lines of troops perform jerky press-ups and jump hurdles. We are days away from the next Bhund. Men on ancient bicycles laden down with buckets, packages – even huge gas canisters – wobble along the road. Rusty tin shacks selling sweets, soda and crisps.

In the river men wash, stripped to the waist, while children skip from stone to stone, cabs sound their horns touting for business; there is a stink of diesel. Shop owners sweep their rubbish from one side to another, women squat in doorways with babies; the scent of garlic, dust, dust and more dust. A line of porters with a three-piece suite on their backs; men with bowed legs and bare feet, schools with names to make you smile – 'Little Angels Prep School,' 'Einstein Academy,' 'Mary Poppins Kindergarten.' Junkyards, water pumps, bare-bottomed babies being washed protestingly under the flowing water and then, abruptly, the mountains soar into sight. The guttural sound of phlegm being cleared, quick, dodge the spit.

I am on a bus bound for Chitwan. Next to me is a Dutch girl on a world tour 'doing' Nepal in two weeks before heading on to China, Laos, Cambodia, Vietnam, Singapore, Australia – yes,yes,yes, I think. That's what I must do next, work my way round this side of the world. Bright tropical flowers and vivid green rice fields pass us on the right, logs by the road, blue plastic awnings on tiny shops. Ugly, heavy furniture stained bilious yellow stands outside a shop; Newari houses, strips of marigolds; seller with tray of eggs, women with prominent nose rings and porters' baskets, fields of hay, mists over the mountains, washing flung over the walls to dry – in the distance brick chimneys belching out smoke. It is 6am – I shudder.

We reach a checkpoint. Sellers with metal bowls full of charred sweetcorn come touting for business; we are at the limits of the city. The bus engine protests as we start to climb up past the corrugated terraces, grey brown and arid, the road giving way to loose shale at the edges. There are death-defying bends. Are we safe? Probably not. Buses plunge down these slopes far too frequently. Palm trees, houses seemingly growing out of the side of the mountain. I doze. At 11.00am we stop for a meal break. The temperature has risen perceptibly.

The scenery has given way to lush plains and palms and more traditional thatched village houses covered in a terracotta wash. We pass through small rural villages with a central tap, chickens, goats, small shops – all the bustle of life in rural Nepal. As we travel southwards the heat intensifies and the vegetation becomes more tropical. I think I must have sweated several pints of water by now. Eventually we reach the outskirts of Chitwan and the bus grinds to a halt in the heat of midday. The traffic snakes ahead endlessly. We are in a copse of trees but, within minutes, there are corn sellers, melon sellers and cucumber sellers who patrol the traffic waiting for the heat to entice some custom. We are there for an hour. It is the army checkpoint.

Eventually our turn for inspection arrives and the Nepalis file off the bus to go through a personal checkpoint. The tourists stay on the bus and look uncomfortable. Cleared by the 'embussing centre' it is only a short distance to Sauraha where the bus terminates on the north side of the National Park.

Eager faces line up by the coach, thrusting business cards at the window. I am already pre-booked at the 'Jungle Safari' Hotel and eventually find the jeep that is picking me up with a rather surly Spaniard and his personal guide. The jeep stalls and a Saddhu, seeing a window of opportunity, grabs the back of the van asking for alms. I select some small grubby notes and he helps push-start the jeep. The hotel is 15 minutes of bumpy drive away and we manage 10 minutes of the journey before we break down again. I hop out, pleased to take the opportunity to stretch my legs. The driver goes to take my bag, but I can see he is already loaded up and I indicate I will carry my own. I see the Nepali guide gesture to the Spaniard and he hands over his bulky rucksack for this little bloke, half his size, to carry. I decide I do not like him.

The hotel consists of individual chalets with straw roofs and verandas grouped round a tropical garden which has a very inviting hammock slung between two trees. The dinning room is a larger hut over to one side. There is a blessedly cold shower in my room and I stand under it for a good long time.

After lunch, we take our first walk into the jungle for a quick look at some of the vast array of plants, many with medicinal properties and for a quick visit to the animal information centre, which has, among other things, photos of animal skat. The significance of identifying different animal shit becomes apparent the following morning when we take a walk in the jungle. We also pay a visit to the elephant breeding centre.

There are two main species of elephant. The Asian species is smaller than the African one, with ears on average three times smaller than the African, but it has more toes. Both species grow 8 sets of four teeth during their lifetime. When the final pair falls out the animal starves to death. In the meantime they eat huge quantities of vegetation which they forage for, but at this centre the elephants are also fed 'elephant sandwiches' which consist of wild rice, sugar and salt bound together in elephant grass, to provide them with essential minerals. The elephant grass, aptly named, grows wild in the park to a height of 8-9 feet.

Elephants have a gestation period of between 19 and 22 months, and although they come into heat annually, they average only a single calf every 3 to 4 years, though they can have offspring up until they are 50 years old. The other thing our guide tells us is that elephants are frightened of ants because they can crawl up inside their trunk and eat their way into the animal's brain (I can remember being frightened by similar tales of earwigs as a child). For that reason elephants sleep with their trunk inside their mouth. Later, when we see termite mounds four to five foot high I am not surprised they are frightened!

Tea is a bleak affair. The dining room houses only me, the surly Spaniard who has not addressed a word to me, and his guide. The hall has a seating capacity of 60 and the waiter tells me that this time last year they had a full house. I ask for gin and tonic but they have no gin. I settle for tonic. After tea we are met by the tour guide who is to take us to 'the cultural programme.'

We walk out in the pitch dark and almost into a barbed wire barrier that has been slung across the road. The guide explains there is a 6pm curfew and no vehicles are allowed down the road after that time. There is a large army camp in the vicinity and the Maoists are active in the region, hence the lack of tourists.

The venue is five minutes' walk down a lane, a long tin hut, which announces itself as a cultural centre. It has wooden benches in rows like a small tin chapel. As usual there is considerable delay before anything happens. I am relieved when the place starts to fill up until the hall is eventually packed.

Having been forewarned that they had not arrived, most of the company finally make it through the roadblocks. We seem to have the full complement of dancers and the standard is uniformly high. The undoubted highlight is a peacock dance where the dancer is doubled up in a very convincing costume. At the end we are invited on to the stage to take part and I join in the dancing.

I return with the others and retire to the chalet and bed – we have a long jungle walk tomorrow morning. I have decided I don't like being a tourist much. It seems a bit pointless to be visiting somewhere just to take a short superficial look at it. If I am to travel further afield I want it to be as a volunteer or a worker. I have lost the taste for just going places to see them, photograph them, tick them off some list and go home again. The guy with the guide doesn't seem to be having much fun doing that either.

Saturday April 20th

We assemble at 6.00am for the walk. 'Is it safe?' I ask, having read reports that it isn't safe to walk through the jungle. 'Yes,' says the guide and then proceeds to alarm me with a list of 'what to do' tips should we encounter the following animals. I pass them on for those interested.

Sloth bears – If they attack, holler like hell – they don't like noise – signs of their presence are deep holes by trees – they dig up and eat certain tree roots.

Rhinos – Have good hearing and sense of smell (not a place to dab on the Chanel) but terrible eyesight. It is why they have the reputation for being aggressive since, being a bit myopic, they wisely operate on the policy that they should charge at anything that comes into view, just in case it is hostile. Mountain bikes send them crazy apparently. Should they charge at you, you have several possible options:-

1 Climb a tree
2 Stand behind a very large one
3 Run in zig zags – they can't cope with that
4 Drop something – they will attack that first

Tigers – They are nocturnal and tend to stay far away from areas with tourists but, in the unlikely event… maintain eye contact at all times and back away very s-l-o-w-ly.

We enter the park after a row down the river in a canoe carved from a single tree – there is room for about 8 people or a combination of people and bikes – several canoes ferrying across the water carry both. As we pass the steep banks we can see many tiny holes which are the nesting places for hundreds of varieties of bird. We see egrets, storks and woodpeckers. Twenty minutes downstream we spot, or rather the guide spots, a crocodile, and the canoe reverses to get a closer look. As we get closer I find myself saying brightly, 'They don't attack canoes, do they?' Suddenly the crocodile rears pretty well alongside us and swims off.

Relief. It's a Galadriel crocodile and they are fish-eating, their snouts so long and thin are incapable of consuming anything larger, but they are strange-looking creatures.

As we enter the jungle we keep alert for the signs we have been told to look for and it's then you realise why skat (shit) spotting can be important. Every skat pile is different – tiger skat is different from deer – a distinction that is worth knowing. Not much doubt which one was produced by elephants; what else could produce such copious quantities?

There are 40 species of snakes in the jungle including cobras and pythons. I am delighted to report we saw none of them. What we did see were tiny white and huge brown butterflies, deer, monkeys, a wild chicken, and our first rhino, which we circle with considerable caution. There are a number of pits dug by sloth bears and we see tiger footprints by the water hole – we even hear a low growling in the undergrowth, which we are told is a tiger, but that is all.

The guide explains the medicinal properties of some of the plants that we pass, for reducing temperature and treating wounds. One plant folds up as you stroke it. A very large rhino crosses our path later in the walk but a further hunt produces no more sightings. Their horns are not as big as their African cousins but they are still not immune from poachers due to the phenomenal sums of money paid for the supposed aphrodisiac qualities contained in ground rhino horn.

As our trek ends we walk through a profusion of tiny yellow butterflies. They remind me of the semi-mythical character in *100 Years of Solitude* who walked with a cloud of them above his head wherever he went. Back by the river we return on the water ferry with a cargo of bikes.

One quick shower later – I think I will need about six in a day, it is so intensely humid here – we are asked if we would like to go and bathe the elephants. It sounds intriguing. I have had one shower but don't mind another so I get into a swimming costume and some trousers and we go into the grounds, where a small elephant is waiting. We are given a chair to ascend and just as I am wondering how that will help, the trainer gives a command and the elephant sinks to its knees. I struggle up on to the animal's back with some difficulty and a few hefty shoves from below. Just as you think you are centrally astride, the creature gets to its feet and you find yourself slipping down one side at a precipitous angle. With the Nepali guide behind me (his companion is having a rest) and the elephant driver in front of me, we reach some sort of equilibrium.

We are riding bare back and it is not very comfortable. The creature has a long bony spine and there are thick spiky hairs on its body that prick into you like wire wool. As we lumber down toward the bank, two of that rare species – tourists – train a video on us. The animal reaches the water and doesn't stop. It plunges in with us on its back. The trainer slides off – it looks a long way down. At a command, the elephant fills his trunk in the river and, flicking it backwards, hoses us down vigorously first on the right then on the left. Its fine at first but then he starts to suck up grit from the riverbed and we find we are being hosed with wet sand.

The trainer gives another command. The animal kneels suddenly catapulting us into the water with a bang. Luckily it is very shallow but there is a strong undertow. We have to look sharp, because the animal just as suddenly rolls on its side and I get out seconds before being flattened by several ton of elephant. We are urged to splash the elephant, which looks well happy to be rid of us and soaking all over in cool water: so relaxed in fact that its bowels suddenly open and we find ourselves in the midst of vast quantities of floating elephant shit.

Thanks to the strong current it floats off fairly fast but I decide to wade as far away from the polluted area as possible and swim with the local women and children. The women watch with some concern as I peel off my dripping trousers and reveal lily-white legs. Observing local dress norms has meant that my legs have not tanned at all. I don't care – I can't swim in trousers.

The water is very refreshing. In the distance, over the sandbanks, comes a cart drawn by two water buffalo. As they near the river they quicken their step and plunge in up to their belly pulling the cart behind them. The cartwheels stick in the mud. On the back of the cart is a Downes Syndrome girl in a wheelchair. Her companion puts a flap down at the back of the cart and manoeuvres her chair on to dry land. It is the first time I have seen someone in a wheelchair in Nepal out and about enjoying some leisure. Facilities for disabled people seem conspicuous by their absence.

The Spanish-speaking guide reminds me that the water is far from clean and that they are ready to turn back for lunch. I have some difficulty getting back on the elephant for the return trip and the trainer leaves me to lead it back all the way to the hotel.

After lunch there is another elephant ride. This time the four elephants have harnesses – thick hessian seats and a contraption that looks like an upturned table on their back. Everyone is advised to sit with legs straddling either side of one of the wooden legs. There are four people to each elephant. I am with a group of Danes who are reasonably interesting and friendly. One elderly woman has been a sister in a nursing home in Lalitpur, can speak Nepali and knows Shuvatara well.

I am getting used to the lurching gait and find the view from the elephants back is excellent. I appreciate how fleet footed they are when my elephant breaks into a run and overtakes the one in front. I feel much safer than on foot, apart from the fact that I am that much closer to snakes in the trees, We pass into the park and within ten minutes, we spot a rhino; it's a great thrill to be so close. Then another in an open clearing, then another bathing in a water hole. With four elephants moving towards it, the rhino in the water gives a bellow of rage and the elephant trainers back off, though it is rare for a rhino to charge elephants, wisely recognising their superior size. I feel quite sorry for the poor thing having to put up with a constant stream of tourists gawking at it. Despite feeling like we are visitors to a theme park, the risks are real for all that. The elderly nurse tells me they had a patient who had been terribly gored by a rhino and its not many years since a guide was trampled to death when acting as decoy for a charging rhino.

We pass through a section of the forest scorched by fire and it is here we see dozens of termite mounds. The return journey takes us through part of the village where all the houses are made traditionally from a base of bamboo and elephant grass covered with yellow clay, mixed with elephant dung, and finished with an orange wash.

We return to the gloominess of an empty hotel. I go for an evening stroll down to the river and cause consternation asking for a gin at a local bar. A key is summoned and then, from out of a very small cupboard, an equally small bottle of Jawalakhel gin is produced. They do know how to make me feel decadent. Strolling back I am amazed to see among the bootleg tapes in a ramshackle tin shack a copy of Neil Simon's *The Capeman.* It bombed on Broadway after only seven performances two or three years ago and (with the exception of Manchester Youth Theatre) has never been staged since. Yet here it is in a shack in the middle of a jungle in South East Asia – how extraordinary is that!

Sunday April 21st

The ride back is uneventful in the sense we don't plunge over any edges, but I am hankering to get back. I feel I should not have gone. There is so much to do. I have seen Chitwan but it has been a hot, muggy experience and I don't really feel any better for it. I am glad to get back to the dust of Kathmandu and to focus on getting this production together.

Sunil's report on progress is worryingly negative and, with a five day Bhund due to start on Tuesday, we have a lot to get sorted on Monday. The Bhund, however, will give me a chance to tackle press releases, organise tickets, contact the media, draw up circulation lists and mail the local schools to ensure we have an audience in the Royal Nepal Academy. Sunil says the venue has a seating capacity of 800 and I am quietly panicking about filling it.

Monday April 22nd

Building work - our rehearsal space vanishes

My daughter Julia's birthday – I must find time to e-mail her some greetings. I arrive at 8am to find Shyam, Rani's husband in the hall with some workmen. Why doesn't anyone tell us what is going on? The children are hovering on the edge of the hall – he sees me, acknowledges me but continues to talk without any recognition that we are booked to use this space. Except, come to think of it, who books anything here?

Twenty minutes after the rehearsals are due to start Shyam leaves and we can get under way, but the punctual pupils have now vanished. By the time I have played sheep dog we have wasted an hour. The group assembled, Sunil takes the rag pickers group and I take the more challenging girls' trafficking group. In the afternoon I take the difficult 'bricks' group, Sunil the domestics. Not that I am complaining too much as I recognise I am better at disciplining some of the school children and I also recognise it is Sunil who can magic it onto the stage and he knows it. We need each other. I don't let him off completely. I ask him to sit in the discussion with the brick makers group while we look at their objections. The main objection is that, if this is the story of child labourers, why are we including the story of a family? I say for various reasons:-

1) Their research provides bare bones but no stories.
2) It is important to recognise that not all children are estranged from their parents if they become child labourers.
3) Thirdly, this is a story of child labour unrecognised – children work in family groups without the cost of their labour being counted. I want to highlight the plight of bonded labour and how it affects the children of the family.

There is silence. 'Are you convinced now?' asks Sunil, who could have argued the point in the first place because he already knew my reasoning. The fact is the privileged children of Shuvatara are alien to him. He feels intimidated by them despite his considerable talent and experience. I just treat them as I would any other adolescent and don't let them get away with anything.

I make a visit to the office to remind Anup that we have to book and pay for the Royal Nepal Academy in cash, plus a returnable deposit, by the end of the day. I am assured everything is set up. We finish rehearsals early to get to the venue by 4pm – they are shutting up at 4.30. I visit the accounts office and ask for the 54,000 rupees required. The accountant glowers at me. I remind him that, thanks to my initiative, he was given a cheque for 110,000 rupees last week, and that the money is not the school's. I explain that if he does not release this money we cannot book the venue.

I am told he can do nothing without Rani's agreement and Rani is in a meeting. I explain that Rani knows all about this and that if the money is not produced in the next ten minutes it will be too late. We have already lost the first date we wanted due to the ILO's inaction. We now have the second date in jeopardy. The accountant, still glowering, marches off to the main school. Eventually with the minutes ticking away, I go and meet him. He is striding back with a look like thunder brandishing a cheque made out in my name.

I explain, yet again, that the money has to be in cash and that with no bank account in Nepal, a cheque made out to me is worthless. We have 35 minutes till the RNA closes. Sunil has been waiting patiently to run us down there on the motorbike. He rings the venue, explains the situation, negotiates for us to pay the following Monday and then he is off. Five minutes after he departs I have the cash. It was in the accountant's drawer all the time. I should by now be used to the 'Nepali way' of doing things, but I am not in the mood to be amused.

I make amendments to the script and take a draft letter to be sent to neighbouring schools down to the office. Chandreyan, wanting to be part of things, attempts, but is persuaded out of, making unnecessary additions.

Rani asks me if I want to go to a wedding – she can see I am cheesed off about the money situation. I say yes – I could do with some relaxation.

I go back and write and write. The Bhund is a godsend in some ways. I go over to the school to send a birthday e-mail to my daughter Julia but the power is down so I make a rather unnerving trip down to the cyber shop in the dark. I spend an evening writing and fall into bed late.

Tuesday April 23rd

I wake early to use the Bhund productively. For a week I will be confined to the house. I have been warned to keep out of town because things could get violent, so I spend the morning writing a Press release for our production.

Under the heading 'Street Children and School Children Act Together for Change' I describe the production and why it is important, that child labour is a global problem with more than one third of the child population of Nepal affected. 'They are the unnoticed, unrepresented, malleable section of the population whose contribution to the support of their families too often goes unrecognised or is dismissed as part of 'culture' of the country,' I write.

I point out the challenge of tackling this immense issue with a huge cast and with less than three weeks' rehearsal period – the Bundh has reduced the potential rehearsal time by five days – and offer my own thoughts about the production:

'It has been an invaluable learning process not just for the pupils but for me too. I shall be returning to the UK much wiser about the issue of child labour and with a real determination to get involved in supporting campaigns in my own country.'

I include a quote from Sunil and some comments from the ILO. Mr Yadav Amatya, National Programme Manager for ILO/IPEC said, 'The theatre project is an experiment by the ILO to determine whether it is possible to produce a lasting change in the attitudes of Nepali children to the effect that child labour is a social evil.We hope to show them that if they want they can bring about a major social change in the country.'

It is when I phone Rani for a quote that I get a flea in my ear. 'Where were you last night?' she asks somewhat imperiously. I explain I went out to send an e-mail to my daughter because it was her birthday. I wonder why she is making such a big thing about it. 'You could have got mixed up in anything,' she says. I let that go.

She eventually tells me I have missed the wedding that I thought was tonight. I am suitably apologetic. What a stupid mistake. I have been so absorbed in work I have not been thinking about anything else. 'We waited some time,' she says in a hurt voice. I have made a major social blunder here and apologise again. I agree to meet later to discuss the Press release. When I do go over at lunchtime, Rani is alone. Chandreyan has gone off to East Nepal for a holiday with his family, but there is much activity in the hall. The team of builders are busy bricking in all the windows along the side of the Hall.

I know that a child broke one of the lower windows but this seems a bit extreme until I notice they are knocking openings for other windows on the opposite side of the building. Since we cannot call a rehearsal till Sunday I figure it may be ready in time, as I have seen the long hours the labourers work here. They are on site very early and are still working under lights when I leave, even on a late night at 7.00 or 8.00pm.

Rani suggests various amendments to the Press release. Niamh, the second Vice-principal, as quiet as Chadreyan is noisy, sits down with a pile of magazines and papers and draws up a list of the media for us to contact. I am amazed they have not got a Press list, given the number of events they organise, and it is a slow process. Nearly every contact has to be telephoned to ask for a fax or e-mail number.

I dissuade Rani from block-advertising, because of the expense. I have the same concerns about the ticket price which Rani wants to set at 450 rupees. I am not sure that under the terms of the grant we are supposed to make a charge, but even if we are, should there not be a concessionary price? I point out that many of the people we would hope to invite could not afford 450 rupees and I am not sure we will be good enough to justify this kind of admission charge. Eventually I persuade her to drop the ticket price to 250 rupees for adults and 100 rupees for children. Is the money going to get re-cycled back to the project? I do not know.

Wednesday April 23rd - Saturday April 26th

I work so hard this week in my Maoist enforced exile that I literally forget what day of the week it is. I write a letter to schools, which Rani redrafts, telling me to paraphrase the Press release or 'no-one will read it'. During my trips into school I keep an anxious eye on what is happening with the hall. Windows that last week were being blocked in are now being knocked out again and windows that were knocked out are now being filled in. Is this some crude exercise in Keynesian economics or just bad planning?

Halfway through the week the labourers start building internal brick walls across the hall and it is only then I discover the hall is being converted into three classrooms. 'But where are we to rehearse?' I ask. No one will answer the question. Finally Rani suggests the large covered area behind the building I live in. I think it over. It has a tin roof, is the same size as the hall and is open to the elements on three sides. The hall has been oppressively hot lately so a cooler space is welcome, despite being susceptible to floods.

However within a few days the newly designated rehearsal space has filled up with desks and a fleet of painters have been dragooned in to paint them pale green. I phone Ashok at the school and ask if the desks can be moved for our rehearsal tomorrow. He comes round in half an hour. 'I have found you a new space, Miss,' he says.

I follow him over to the pre-school building. He shows me a small, covered veranda in front of the nursery. Two guard dogs in kennels bark continuously when they see us and there is noise from the road. I ask him if the classes are let out onto the veranda, mindful that in a week's time the children are back after their long school holiday (our team have been working through their break). He says they do. I reject the space and ask for the original area to be cleared as it is only two days from our resumption for rehearsals. 'But it is Sunday tomorrow, Miss,' says Ashok.

I am deeply distressed. I have lost a day. I was certain it was Friday. I must redouble my efforts now. I have been working like an automaton, up at 5am working till summoned by the school then back to writing until late. I have seen no one and have gone nowhere apart from two early morning walks around Sanepa to clear my head.

I had got in food supplies for the week thinking the Bhund would close everything, but I note from my walks this is not the case. Most small food stores are open, selling fresh vegetables, eggs, rice and other basics. They would have to be, a week's inactivity would probably wipe most of them out. Besides, this is a population that has no convenience food and little or no cold storage.

Sunday April 27th – Friday 2nd May
Run-up to performance

Some of the children reassemble for a rehearsal on Sunday. The desks have been moved and the floor is filthy. I asked the security guard if he could sweep the floor but he has ignored me. If I had a brush I would have done it myself. The rag pickers' rehearsal goes well. They are a tight, self-disciplined group.

The other three plays are a very long way from being ready. Arniko, playing the brother in the girls' trafficking story, is beginning to settle down a bit but Probalata is finding the role of the pregnant sister very taxing. She stops whenever there is the necessity for an emotional response and either rolls her eyes or screws them up and breathes heavily. I try to convince her that if she feels the emotion inside, the body language will fall into place naturally.

I sit down with her. ‘What,’ I ask, ‘is the worst thing that has ever happened to you?’ She thinks long and hard. ‘The possibility I will fail my exams?’ she offers finally. I am not surprised she is having problems with this part, though I do not for a minute underestimate the seriousness with which examinations are taken in Nepal. They are one of the main ways of ensuring you maintain your social position and it’s a long way down from the top here – all the way down to the brothels of Mombai. Thankfully this sweet, conscientious girl will never be faced with such an appalling future. Then again, she will almost certainly not choose acting as a career, though I do think she is one of those for whom this experience will be deeply felt and for whom there may be a lasting impact.

I think however, she is in a minority. We are working with some competent, organised, even outstanding pupils, but they are few and far between. The majority are just plain hard work and a few are deliberately obstructive. They come late, they whine to go home early. I remind myself they are also adolescents. I talk to Sunil many times about their motivation. ‘They are not serious about this thing,’ he says. We start timetabling them a group at a time so that we can direct together.

We experiment, we swap parts, and I rewrite sections of the script and narration. There is a scene at the end of the domestics’ story where Aalishma playing the domestic, has to mime various household tasks showing the increasingly frantic efforts of the domestic to keep up with the demands of the household. She cannot get the movements right. This is a girl that has never in her life hung washing on a line or chopped vegetables. Interestingly, the school children have largely chosen to play the part of the child labourers, whereas some of the children from CWIN are enjoying ordering them about as employers!

They start to bring in what they think are suitable costumes for their part. It is often what they think they look attractive in. We ponder over the right thing for the brick workers and the prostitutes to wear. The inappropriateness of some of the costumes suggests they are not picking up the right messages. I get more and more irascible by the day.

I bring in the backstage crew on Monday and explain all the props that need to be made and enlist the help of the art teachers making 'bricks' out of blocks of polystyrene. One day finds me and two pupils crawling around in the space below the roof where they keep old costumes from previous productions, while doves fly in and out of a large, unshuttered circular window just above our heads. I spend my evenings making props lists and agitating for things.

One night I cycle to the shops in the dark – always a hazardous undertaking. On my return a local dog chases me as I near the school. I increase my speed – the dog keeps pace with me. His excited barking attracts another dog who joins in the chase, and another and another and another. Soon half the dogs in Sanepa are after me. I lunge out wildly, trying to kick the nearest mutt on the nose which is a mistake. My bicycle hits a boulder and then I am flying over the handle bars. Great, I think, first time in your life you have a chance to direct a piece of theatre and before it can happen, what do you end up as? Dog-meat.

I land badly in a pile of dirt and wait to be engulfed by half-starved dogs. However my spectacular sail through the air frightens the hell out of the cowardly dogs and they take off into the dark, leaving me to limp back with a smarting elbow and knee, knowing I will have grazes that will ooze for weeks in this humid tropical climate. I use up my store of bandages and plasters, examine my leg where a giant bruise is already appearing, and curse every canine in sight.

Rani decides to call a dress rehearsal she will attend on the Sunday. In the midst of all this I try to coax an opening song out of the musicians. The first attempt is not successful. I suggest it needs to be deeper, with more undertones. They go away for another try. I do not see them all week. I listen to the tune Arniko has supposedly been working on for three weeks with his friend, for the girls' story. It is awful. Sunil and I start talking about soundtrack music …

The rehearsal space floods two or three times and I have to go out there with a mop to get rid of the surplus water. We are still battling with the desk painters for space. I feel totally unsupported. It is clear our project gets low priority at present. I urge all the children to bring their costumes and props for Saturday.

Each evening I find props scattered about the building. Kussum, one of the street children has taken a fancy to a doll used as a prop for the two girls playing young mothers. She has clearly never had a toy of her own and each day she lovingly winds it in a cloth and sits nursing it. Each evening I have problems detaching her from it because I cannot afford to lose any of the props. Each time I feel mean doing so and resolve to buy her a doll of her own when this is over.

I have tried to explain to the backstage team that they are responsible for clearing up after the performers, but they just push off and ignore me. One girl goes off in a huff and can't even be bothered to tell me she has dropped out. It is because she suggested I should do some of the backstage jobs and I just exploded. I think my intolerance is partly due to stress, but also because I feel they take so much for granted. Part of the learning curve for them is doing work they consider beneath them – it is one more way I worry that the message of the play is not getting through. Sunil doesn't help by refusing to take decisions about rehearsal times, which often means I have to do a nightly ring round to summon them for rehearsals the following day.

Saturday May 3rd

Rani arrives at 12.30pm for the dress rehearsal and wants to know if we have eaten. The last thing I want to do is to break for lunch now or we will never get them assembled again. There are problems with the costumes. Aalishma who is playing the domestic still keeps arriving in a shalwa kemise in pale pastel colours with a long, flowing, white chiffon scarf. I point out (yet again) she could not scrub floors in that outfit. She listens politely and then asks if she has to change it. I want to scream. The following day she comes with a maroon floaty scarf – is this progress?

Prayas, playing Dil the brick worker's son, comes dressed in a pair of bright yellow Shuvatara running shorts and brilliantly white vest. Where is the longhi and the brick-stained vest he promised he would bring? He says he hasn't got a longhi and promises for about the fourth time, he will bring in a suitably distressed, dirty vest. I cannot help thinking that the pristine vest is probably the product of another child's laundering.

Christina, playing the older sister in the brick workers story, wants to know if she has to wear the dress I have 'distressed' in the art department, splattering it liberally with grey paint so that it will look like she spends her life in close proximity to raw clay. Probalta playing a girl who is supposed to be heavily pregnant refuses to wear a cushion because it ruins the line of her sari. Instead she looks like a Vogue model.

The rehearsal gets underway. Rani is impressed with the rag pickers. 'Is there more?' she asks. 'Don't hold your breath,' I say. 'It's downhill all the way after this.' As the girls' trafficking story starts, I tell her it's a true story. 'Surely not,' she says. 'It couldn't have been her brother who sold her, it must have been her step-brother.' I assure her it is the blood brother who sold his sister. I wonder about this demonisation of step-parents – 7% of trafficked girls are sold by an immediate relative. I have been getting very bothered about how great the level of ignorance is among people who would normally regard themselves as well-informed. I have to keep reminding myself that there is plenty of ignorance about homelessness in the UK too. Whatever society we live in, it is possible for people with affluence to 'pass by on the other side'. How much do I know about life on the street in Britain?

Rani is impressed, but worried we have had no food. She says she thinks the play is great and that I am too close to see it – the children are feeling it, she is sure of that. 'You are going to take Nepal by storm, I know it,' she says to them all before telling them to concentrate on what Hazel Miss tells them. Sunil and I had been planning to challenge them about why they were doing this, because some of them seemed insensitive to the issues. However, I noticed a perceptible lift when they had Rani to perform to.

This is just one production, and I am one Westerner trying, with however many good motives, to crash through centuries of tradition – some good, some bad. While I have been trying to beat the clock, the school has had other priorities. As well as a major building operation, evicting us from our former rehearsal space, over the last week the basketball pitch at the school has been covered with a multi-coloured awning, making a vast enclosed tent. An elaborate altar has been built on the stage and I am told the school premises are being offered as a centre for devotional prayer and religious and moral debate. A small open fire has been built at one end of the playground and loudspeakers at the end of the road call devotees to puja several times a day.

Rushing into school for props or to find the music teacher I frequently arrive as the call for prayer relays out of the speakers and find I am dodging between devotees, walking at a slow and measured pace towards the school gates. The majority are women carrying small brass trays with offerings of fruit, flowers and tikka paste.

Watching them I am aware of the centuries-old belief system that beats like a pulse through this hot and troubled land. It is a salutary reminder that my role here is transient and that what we are engaged in has a rhythm and energy quite apart from these ancient rituals and customs. Many of the pupils arrive to rehearsal with a red tikka spot on their forehead and towards the end of the rehearsal period one of the 16-year-old musicians disappears for a day to have his head shaved and adopt the saffron robes of a priest as a kind of rite of passage to adulthood.

Sunday May 4th - Wednesday May 7th

I live and breathe rehearsals, my room gets more and more untidy and so does the building we are working in. I make props. Everything is last-minute. Sunday all the children return, so the Principal and Vice-Principal are distracted. We have made a stack of bricks out of polystyrene and poor Christina Shrestha who has never rehearsed carrying them before suddenly finds she has this huge unwieldy prop. 'It's too big for her,' says Pranjali (who plays the brick worker's wife), 'can't we cut it down a bit?' 'I would have thought that was precisely the point we are trying to get across, Pranjali,' I say. 'She is only carrying polystyrene. How would she have felt if it was real bricks?'

I agitate for a screen for the brothel scene endlessly. On Tuesday Chandreyan summons me to view a huge bulky thing the carpenter has built out of filthy old scrap wood. It is three times too big and almost unliftable even when they remove a section. I explain that I do not want 'four strong men to lift it into position', it has to be carried on discreetly and quickly by two 14-year-old girls. I despair. I have run out of time and there is still much to do. Why could we not buy a cheap screen? Where has our props budget disappeared to? Good question.

Rani tells me she knows I have standards but this is Nepal and things do not work like that here. I apologise for my irascibility. She gives me a hug. I am close to tears and very, very tired. Beejay from the school office comes to the rescue on Tuesday, goes out shopping with my list and comes back with exactly what I need. He gets a special vote of thanks for keeping me sane and understanding what is required.

Left alone in the blistering midday sun while the pupils disappear to the puja and Sunil flies to the sound studio to record special effects, I tack the bright, gaudy material Beejay has bought to cover the screen with the heavyweight frame and then attend to the final programme details.

The shock is the number of tickets we have sold. If the VP has his calculations right, I,200 tickets have been sold – Sunil has underestimated the capacity. We now have both downstairs and upstairs jammed and a Government Minister is due to attend.

On Tuesday we receive a visit from the Director of the ILO/IPEC project in Geneva, Maria Gabriella Lay. She is here to see the first ever SCREAM production in Nepal and only the second in the world. There has been one in Ireland, but not on this scale, and the Irish delegate has also flown over to see it. She comes and takes tea on my roof and quizzes Sunil and me about how we have put this production together. She is wearing the simplest of white linen suits which I am confident will have cost double the amount that I have lived on for the last 3 months. I begin to become aware that we are dealing with people who operate in very influential international circles, the big players.

The true nature of what we have taken on hits me. We have been pioneering a programme that has international significance, that may pave the way for many future international developments. I am also somewhat daunted by the responsibility. How good has my understanding been of what they want? There are so many loose ends.

Thursday May 8th
Dress Rehearsal

The dress rehearsal at the RNA is disastrous. There are problems getting the children used to wearing stage mikes and, as there are only a few, Sunil has worked out a complicated rota for their use.

Gunga, one of the CWIN girls playing the brothel Madam, is resplendent in a loaned green and gold sari. She loves wearing make up and jewellery to such an extent that she does not want to take off her costume for the last scene where she has to re-appear as a rural peasant, and has taken to hiding till seconds before her final appearance. I warn the backstage team they must intercept her!

We have no props table or side lights backstage, so props are all over the place. Sunil is in the lighting box struggling with the lighting system so I have to orchestrate the mayhem on stage. In the absence of anything more sophisticated, we communicate via a loud hailer. Rani is right. The vast barn of a place does smell of wee. I go home in a state of terror and write notes into the small hours for the essential morning run-through.

Friday May 9th
D-Day

I am up at 4am making lists and writing instructions as I need to put my backstage team in the hands of two volunteer teachers. I need to be in the orchestra pit to cue Gunga, the technician, for the PowerPoint presentation and the video. He has done it all of once.

Each of the four sections of the play will be followed by some silent statistics rolling up on a screen at the back of the stage giving the facts and figures about the children in each industry. The statistics have been checked and the PowerPoint prepared by the ILO for which I am extremely grateful.

We are at the hall by 10am and everyone is in costume by 10.30. Then all the mikes fail. The technician is summoned while we struggle through the ill-rehearsed opening song. It is sung in Nepali and only translates very loosely along the lines of the lyrics I wrote. Broadly translated the words have taken on a more spiritual tone in the hands of the music teacher, but the music is haunting and evocative and sets the scene well.

The rivers are flowing with shame
They're equal. They all sound the same
They flow the way human life flows
All of us are equal but our fates are different

In darkness they are lost and sold
There is no light around them
Their life is nipped in the bud

Don't sell the girls
Stop child labour
One person should not suppress another

Human greed leads to brutality
Work for others and please the gods
If there was equality
This world would be heaven

Problems with the mikes continue and during an early break I take the opportunity to talk to Ray Conway from SCREAM in Ireland. Amazingly he has been impressed by what he has seen – this is the first time he has felt an authentic connection has been made. He is concerned that so many of the international delegations that visit places like Nepal rarely leave the ersatz environment of the luxury hotels and go home without any real feeling or understanding of the issues or the country they have visited. He says that he would love to see this production visiting Ireland, and our young people meeting up with the young people they have worked with, who have been drawn from a mix of religions, social classes, city and rural areas. We talk enthusiastically about the possibilities of doing just this. He says he will talk to Ms Lay about it.

By 12.00 the mikes are still not quite fixed and I am shitting bricks. I track Sunil down and find him calm and unperturbed. 'It will be all right,' he says, 'there is no time for a dress rehearsal now. It would take their energy away from the main performance.'

I know he is right but the prospect still seems alarming. I gather my little backstage team together. They stare at me with frightened eyes while I tell them it's all down to them now and take them through every last detail. I hope I have delivered a suitable rallying cry. They look as if I have just asked them to leave the trenches, go over the top and face enemy gunfire.

At 1.00pm Rani arrives with a whole team of Front of House reinforcements to give out programmes and to help the various NGOs who are setting up exhibitions in the foyer. I have put tickets on the door for Sarah (Lorna has already returned to the UK) Ram and all the children, Rajan and Bhakta, whom I have neglected for some weeks. We have one Cabinet Minister for certain attending, representatives from all the major NGOs in Nepal and dozens of school parties. Our school has arranged a banner across the drive and Nepalaya are in position to film the whole thing for posterity.

The performance was nothing short of a miracle, because something quite magical happened on that stage a couple of hours later. Those kids came on stage and they acted their socks off. The backstage made only one smallish boob in the whole play. The atmosphere was electric. 800 schoolchildren in the audience did not even so much as rustle a paper bag.

I am like a coiled spring, in a constant state of tension, but as the play unrolls I suddenly know very clearly what I am very, very good at and should have been doing years ago, because I can see the play visibly making an impact. I can feel it quite tangibly. Chandreyan keeps appearing from the audience muttering, 'It's going very, very, well.'

The rag pickers piece, our tour de force, goes splendidly, but so does the girls' story. The musicians, at the last moment, have come up with the most touching Newari song to accompany the funeral procession for the baby in the brick makers' story. I have never seen the children play this scene properly before. Now they are on the stage and they are so professional I feel a lump come to my throat. They are applying everything I have been pleading with them to do. I had wondered if the staging was at fault, but no, this was exactly the right way to stage it. They just needed to feel it. I want to cry.

The aftermath, flowers, congratulations, go by in a daze. There are speeches on stage, Sunil and I are garlanded with the most elaborate and fancy orange marigolds. Nepalaya want an immediate post-performance response and all I can say is how relieved I am and how fantastic the children are. I am told that one of the most extraordinary things about the performance, which lasted two and a half hours, was that throughout you could hear a pin drop. Did I know, I am asked, how disruptive Nepali school children usually are when they attend performances? The Cabinet Minister has not said a word throughout the performance and has left silently at the end.

I go out front to try and spot Ram and the children but he has left. Rajan and his cousin are there, however, and they are deeply impressed. We arrange to meet one last time before I leave Nepal next week.

Praktikree, one of the Shuvatara children, extracts a promise that I will approach Rani about organising a post-show party for the children on Saturday and I promise to do my best. The children's coach departs. Rani has claimed me for a ride in the limo and we go to Nanglos for a meal with Rita her sister, who presents me with a wonderful bouquet of flowers. I am so very happy and also sad because my return is imminent and I do not want to go. Ms Lay has said she wants the performance repeated for International Labour Day on June 12th and one part of me wants to stay on to oversee a revised version of the play.

Aftermath, Home

I look in vain for reviews of the play in the English-speaking papers. I am shown only two in Nepali. Both have changed the title of the play from 'Rivers of Shame' to 'Rivers of Rome' and neither of the reports mentions the content of the plays. I am told this is quite a common form of censorship in Nepal – censorship by typo. Does this mean we made more impact than was expected? I rather think that it does. I don't know whether to be consoled by the thought or frustrated. Both, I think.

On Friday I am summoned over to the main school and arrive just as all the children are assembled on the baseball pitch. Rani is on the stage with a microphone and gestures me onto the stage for a goodbye speech. I tell them that it has been a privilege to work with them and that I shall never forget this experience. It is true. I am presented with more flowers and a large parcel and many cards. I am hugely embarrassed. 'Aren't you going to open it?' asks Rani. So I do, and I am touched beyond belief. They have had a black Pashmina dressing gown specially made for me. I shall treasure it. I am also presented with a Khukuri knife in a leather sheath by some of the lads from the play. 'What is this for?' I ask. 'Decapitating goats, Miss,' they reply. Not the most obvious present then for a vegetarian, but of great symbolic value to me for all that.

The whole school files onto the platform to say goodbye personally. They press presents and cards and small flowers into my hands. Some are crying. 'Please come back, Miss,' say one or two of my star actors and I know we are going to miss one another greatly. The girls have brought me a Kumari mask and all of them have signed a big bag with their autographs. I think my chances of returning home within the given weight restrictions has been blown.

'Well,' says Rani, 'you will be getting a lot of e-mails. I think you have just acquired 600 children!' I hope so. Later I phone my friends. Sarah had got the day wrong and has not seen the play. I am disappointed. I wanted very badly for someone from back home to have seen my work. Ram and the children did see it and are wildly excited by it. I am invited over to the Centre on Sunday. Rajan and I arrange to meet with his cousin Bhakta on

Monday. I also ask him to invite Madhev and his wife to meet me – we have not seen each other since the wedding. I am harbouring a slim hope that Madhev can utilise his contacts at the airport to perform miracles with my excess luggage.

The real surprise is to come. The school asks me to go to the office where the Vice-Principal solemnly presents me with what seems a very large fee of 25,000 rupees (about £250) and explains that the ILO wants me to have this. I explain that I was not expecting this and did not want it. Although it means I can now buy a decent birthday present for my daughter and perhaps even a flight over Everest, which at 8,500 rupees I had not previously expected to afford, I decide I am not going to pocket the difference.

I meet Shanta, from CWIN, on my way back to the school apartment. He has come to say goodbye. Child Workers in Nepal has impressed me greatly. I have heard that the young actors from CWIN, who have performed so magnificently, are sharing a flat together but that CWIN are having difficulties supporting them. I ask Shanta how much their rent is and there is enough left from my fee to buy them 6 months. I am returning to a well-appointed home and some paid work – however temporary. My life is singularly more blessed than theirs.

That night I visit my second theatre production in Nepal – extracts from The Ramayana, performed at the beautiful Hotel Vajra, up in the hills near Swayambhunath. The hotel comprises several separate traditional buildings facing into a beautiful old courtyard, and has a long tradition of mounting theatre productions and cultural evenings. The large room that serves as a theatre is packed and accessed via a stairwell crammed with photographs of previous productions. It is the first time since I arrived in Nepal that I realise I have stumbled into an environment for theatre that seems familiar. I feel distressed that I should have only just discovered this place on the point of leaving. How much else have I missed?

I have a complementary ticket from the German designer of the production whose child has just entered Shuvatara. She is something of a theatrical force in Nepal and has visited Rivers of Shame. She thought it was good but that it didn't present any real solutions. She is right. There should have been more of that, but my defenders are quick to point out that this is an international problem which has eluded easy solutions for years at government level. How could she expect them to be incorporated in a two-hour production, with a group of children who have never acted before and after only a few weeks' rehearsal? Still, I do think she has a point.

The production is magnificent. The company are from New Delhi and their mime and dance is among the best I have seen, but I am exhausted and am nearly asleep by the end. I join invited guests on the rooftops at the end for a nostalgic view of the old city I have come to love, even though I recognise I hardly know it at all. A party is evolving in a room off the veranda and the eerie sounds of a didgeridoo float up to the rooftops. I am too tired to continue, make my excuses and leave.

Of the rest, perhaps the most significant time is the party for the children on Saturday. It is at the Nanglos near Bhakta's house. When I arrive the majority of the pupils are there. The girls are squeezed into some pretty revealing and stunning clothes and they look utterly beautiful. All the CWIN children and Shanta have got here, despite a last-minute change of venue and Sunil has come with his young son. It is interesting to watch the level of integration now with a performance behind them. Shirjit is a great hit with the CWIN lads and they hang around a fair bit together. Anju, the sweet-faced young singer from the school, has become very motherly toward two of the youngest CWIN girls, one of whom is sitting on her lap.

Rani gathers them all together and we sit round a big, square table while she asks them to tell her what the project has meant for them. Prashamsha, one of my narrators in the play, is one of the first to speak. She says that doing the research on the trafficking of girls has opened her eyes and as a result of her involvement with WOREC she has re-thought her career options. She now wants to train as a social worker specialising in women's issues. Galaxy and Haushala follow. Haushala, particularly, has got on exceptionally well with the young male actors from CWIN. She has had a quite pivotal role in the rag pickers' play and has emerged as a tough and spirited actor. She says that they have both made a decision to become involved with Save the Children's girls' harassment project. She says that sometimes she has felt bored and stifled having been at the same school all her life. Then something like this happens and she is so glad that she is at Shuvatara. Rani is clearly touched.

Other testimonials follow. They have all enjoyed themselves. The CWIN actors say that they are glad they have met the Shuvatara children and have friends now they intend to keep in touch with. Rani muses about whether Shyam should start a soup kitchen for the street children. I squirm a bit and suggest that she donates the money to CWIN instead.

Sunil presents me with a small, carved, wooden picture frame and the two CDs we took our sound track from. I am really touched. I was going to give him my drama games book but forgot it in the rush, so make arrangements to meet him briefly on Monday. I have also bought him a book on Shelley because I know he likes poetry and thought he might like to try something from our radical tradition of poets. I have brought Rani a long poem in a slim volume by Maya Angelou and a book by Tagore.

I feel a bit like the researchers in the first BBC Seven-up programme when they brought their groups of public school and working-class kids together for a party at the end of the programme. The only difference is that my research will stop here and from here on now I will be restricted to whatever I can entice people to send me on an e-mail. Trying to assess how successful this project has been in the long term will not be easy. There is much enthusiasm from all sides for the idea of bringing the parties over to the UK and I hold on to this idea as I leave.

Sunday is busy. I am at the airport by 6am for my early morning flight over Everest. It is bitterly disappointing. I am seated over the wing and see little except a wall of rock in the distance . I am on the wrong side to view Everest and only get a close-up of everyone else's backsides as they cram up to the window. In turns we get one short visit into the cockpit but it is still disappointing. Nothing can compare with trekking the mountains. That experience will stay in my heart forever. I wish I had donated the extra money to CWIN now.

Later I cycle out to Baluwatar Chowk where Ram's colleague is to meet me on his motorbike to guide me back to Chandol. This time the children greet me like an old friend. I have brought over a rucksack of children's games and books and Ram tells me warmly how splendid he thought the production was and how impressed he was at how well I understood and got the children to put the issues across. He says his children watched quite spell-bound.

The house that I thought so bleak on my first visit looks familiar and homely now, though the turquoise paint used to decorate the children's bedrooms is a debatable improvement. Outside, though, the garden is a riot of green vegetation. The pump has been completed and the crops are clearly benefiting. A swing and a see-saw have been donated and are in regular use. There are smiles all round. I read them some stories in English and take some final photographs of the children, then I follow Ram down along the riverbed to his house where they have cooked me a final meal. It is delicious. I vow to bring him over to England in July on a fundraising tour and he promises to contact me and let me know the price of his ticket as soon as he can.

I spend the evening in Thamel with Sabitha and we find a shop selling the Chinese silk dresses I have in mind to buy for Julia but there is none in a size that will fit. The owner insists on making one for the following day and because I don't know if she is a size 14 or a 16, he says he will make it a 15. What amazing service. Sabitha promises to pick it up for me.

The meeting with Rajan and Bhakta the following day is a little uneasy. This is because I have insisted on treating them all to lunch in Thamel. Bhakta has been putting me under a lot of pressure to eat at his house. I am equally determined to be the host this time. This was Bhakta's last chance to get me to agree to sponsor him and there is no getting away from it, he has come, but he is sulking. Rajan greets me with a present the size of a shoe box. My heart sinks. I have done some preliminary packing and am privately worried how an earth I am going to accommodate anything else bulkier then a handkerchief. But how kind to buy me a present which later turns out to be a handcarved Nepalese sarangi – and I can't even play a musical instrument!!

Rajan's uncle Madhev and his wife arrive and present me with a small box of tea and we all have a pleasant lunch in the small, leafy, outdoor terrace of a local restaurant. Madhev offers to come with me to the offices of Quatar Air to negotiate over my surplus luggage and we go on there after lunch. Madhev is magnificent. He sees the manager and explains the work I have been doing in Nepal and that much of my surplus weight will be due to teaching materials and research books. I am assured I will get a generous discretionary allowance. Madhev says he will be at the airport for me tomorrow to ensure there are no hitches.

In fact he leaves me with such confidence over my waived weight restrictions that I ride up to Lazinpath to have my bike dismantled and packed in a bike bag. I want to take it home with me. I have never had such a good and responsive bike in my life. Nima is waiting on my return. He has also bought me a present of a Buddhist prayer scarf. I give him a kiss and a hug under the slightly furtive but amused gaze of the security guard to whom I suspect I have been a source of entertainment for some months. I wish him well as a trek leader. The next person to arrive is Sabitha with the dress. We have both bought each other earrings as a present. I shall really miss her. She filled many a well of loneliness with her wonderful, cheerful presence.

I pack everything as best I can and groan inwardly when I lift the book bag. But there is one more task I have to complete. I know it will be ragged and unformed and needing a huge number of amendments, but I have to finish this book before I leave. I have this suspicion that if I just take a copy on a floppy disc it will prove to be some vagrant strain that refuses to open on a UK computer and I want the satisfaction of printing off those last few pages and wiping the record clean. I do not want to leave my random thoughts behind for curious eyes, because in its first draft there is too much personal stuff I most definitely do not want anyone to view – at least not till I have had a chance to edit some of it out. I have used my writing to express frustrations I would not dream of exposing to public view without a more measured appraisal.

I tell Rani, who has popped across to see me, that I want to spend the evening writing, but she has come to invite me to a coming-of-age party. It is for the young lad who wore the priest robes for a day. His mother is the art teacher who helped me construct the props. I cannot say no. I tell her I will stay up and write all night instead. She thinks I am mad.

The car arrives to whisk me off to an unfamiliar part of the city. On the way Rani tells Shyam about my weight restriction problem and he whips out his mobile and talks to a Mr Thapa. I am told Shyam has fixed it. I explain that an intervention has already been made on my behalf but I am assured Mr Thapa is the man. I am told that if Shyam had known earlier he could have had me upgraded to business class all the way to London, but that this has been arranged now, at least to Doha. I do not know what to say. I personally would be happy to be stowed in an overhead locker with a jam butty if they could just ensure I don't pay through the nose for my library and my bike.

It has been raining and there is a lot of mud underfoot as we slither our way over to the huge marquee set up on open ground near our host's house. Many of the school children are leaving as we arrive. It looks as if the whole school has been invited. I have had a bit of a brainwave and asked Rani if it is customary to bring a present to an event such as this and she says that it is. The lad is a musician. I have found a home for the sarangi. I hope Rajan would not feel too insulted if he knew. I am later reassured by a Buddhist friend who tells me all offerings have a natural home and it is perfectly acceptable to redistribute presents to those who can make best use of them.

This is going to be a long night. During the next hour while we eat and drink, much whisky is consumed by these old friends who all come from the same Newari village. They lapse into rounds of endless folk songs interspersed with the boy's father coming over and clasping my hands in his to tell me how wonderful the play was. He is almost speechless with emotion though the drink may have played a part there. He insists that if I ever return to Nepal, I must be a guest at his house.

His admiration for the play seems clear, until he tells me that the Shuvatara children always rise to the occasion in the end. I had thought the play was more than giving the school children a chance to work on a production with an English and Nepali director, but I am sadly aware how this may become the dominant memory – another glorious first for Shuvatara.

I can hear Sunil's voice in my ear. 'They are not serious, Hazel.' I know it is true. But have we lit a tiny flame in the minds of their children? I hope so. There seems to be a handful of children who have been influenced. Can we really expect more without a continuous programme? And where are the signs that this exists? The only follow-up seems the tentative idea for a tour and I don't know how practicable or possible this is.

I am returned home in the pouring rain at 2am. I set the alarm clock to 4am- I have to be at the airport by 6am. By 4am I am up, shivering in my clothes and blinking at my computer screen and praying no thunderstorm will rob me of my final lines. The rain pours down outside in great, merciless streams. I type on. I leap over the last few weeks in an unsubtle burst and place the final full stop on a completed, but ultimately unsatisfactory, first draft as the call comes up the stairs. I print the last page and place it in the document file, copy it all to a disk and very carefully and deliberately drag my book to the trashcan on the screen and empty it.

Rani has had just four hours' sleep. She has risen to see me off. I am deeply touched. When she hears I have already been up for two hours she tells me I really am mad. Yes, I think, and I intend to stay that way. Life is too short for sleeping when there is so much to do. This has been the most

exhilarating three months I have spent for many years and I want to do it again and again and again. She sees me to the car with the rain pounding on her umbrella. She is my didi bata (little sister), we have shared so many confidences. Our lives are so dissimilar, yet we have found the common thread. I have no doubt she does not share my passions and much of my anger about the injustices I have seen, but she is still an immensely kind and caring woman and I have a lot of love and respect for her. We hug.
'I shall miss you,' she says. And me. I don't know how I can bear to go.

We are very late to the airport. Everything goes disastrously wrong. I miss Mr Lohani, and Mr Thapa, Shyam's contact who is supposed to smooth my path, does exactly the reverse. He demands £998 excess for my luggage, three times more than my total living costs in Nepal and significantly more than the price of a return ticket.

I am near to tears. I explain that I have been working in schools as a volunteer, that much of my luggage is research papers and books and that I don't have that kind of money. He is unmoved. He tells me I can leave things behind. How to calculate that in minutes? I ask them to weigh the bicycle but that saves relatively little, and I cannot leave my books or research papers behind.

Suddenly Mr Lohani is by my side, looking quite desperate and clutching a small bouquet of flowers. I think he is going to burst into tears. 'Where were you?' he says, 'I have looked everywhere.' He has already taken in what has happened but he leaves no stone unturned. He argues long and hard. He goes behind the counter into an inner room and emerges with someone else, still arguing. He stops to tell me he has explained what I have been doing in Nepal. The upshot is they reduce the insane charge I could not, would not pay, to… £450. I am still utterly gutted. I have the strong suspicion that if I had met Mr Lohani earlier none of this would have happened.

'If you had only waited for me,' says Madhev sorrowfully. He has done his best, but it is a sad way to leave after all those highs I have been on. I pay by credit card. He books me into business class to Doha as a consolation and insists on accompanying me through the airport and sitting sorrowfully by my side till my plane is called. His dismay is so palpable, I try my hardest to cheer him up. He shows his security pass to enable him to escort me right to my seat on the plane, and does not leave until the last possible moment. I wish I could make him feel better. I feel I have let him down.

At Doha I meet another disgruntled passenger, a backpacker who has had to pay excess. He says that Qatar air are now offering a bonus to their staff for any excess baggage charges they impose, so their discretionary policies are now blunted by self-interest, and of course it all adds to the airline's coffers.

Ultimately none of this can take away what I have seen, what I have done and what it has done to me. None of that has a price; it is beyond measure. I have been changed as a person and although I do not know what I am going back to or when I will return, this place has turned my heart, tested my resilience and given me a pride and confidence in my abilities that I never had before. It has also made me determined to get involved again, to fight the good fight. There is much to change and I am a natural born campaigner. I can no longer waste time on the sidelines.

Reflections

Despite my best efforts to bring *Rivers of Shame* to the UK, I have run into innumerable problems.

The biggest obstruction, surprisingly, came from the ILO. Our role as pioneers became clear when we discovered that a man we had never met was still producing guidelines for the SCREAM project, who regretted (when I finally tracked him down in Ireland) not being in Nepal for the project due to the 'political instability.' The draft guidelines were produced six weeks after we completed the play. No one at the school had ever heard of him.

The wordy e-mail I eventually received from him, after months of petitioning and when the date had long passed when it was possible to secure UK venues for that Autumn, informed me that both he and the Project Director did not believe the play should be taken out of its cultural context. I was informed the process was the key part of the programme, not the product.

I wrote back saying that I understood this, but without the product the process would not have worked. The children needed a focus to experience the issues so intensely and many of them now wanted the chance to spread the message. The implication that a cultural exchange visit would have no value out of its local context seemed to me to belie much of the philosophy behind the hundreds of educational and cultural bodies worldwide whose central ideology and reason for existence is to promote cultural understanding through precisely these kinds of exchanges.

The Geneva Project Manager duplicated his response word for word. They were adamant they would offer no support for the idea – even moral. By then I had long since enthusiastically offered my support to the ILO in London and told them about the proposed tour hoping to elicit their support. The writer of the guidelines informed me this was 'unfortunate' and that the Geneva office had mailed the London office to tell them not to get involved.

I was later informed that I would be sent a final version of the guidelines and that perhaps I would like to consider more of this work in the UK, although they 'could not consider paying me'. I thought of the Geneva Manager in her designer clothes and declined. Later, when I was asked to write on the outcomes of the project, I contacted the Geneva office to ask if they could give me an example of the 'powerful and sustainable links' which they said had been made on the project. I did not get an answer. Visiting their website early in 2004 I discovered the guideline writer now had a prestigious job in the Geneva office of IPEC. I contacted them again and asked for the material they promised to send me. They agreed to do so. It never arrived.

The school was the next to withdraw, citing exams, but the same day that I received this disappointing response from the Principal, the children relayed a message from the Vice-Principal asking if I had raised the money for the tour yet. I continued to get mixed messages, as if they hadn't made a final decision. Finally, after asking for an unambiguous answer, I got an abrupt and abrasive response from Rani telling me to stop troubling them. That really hurt.

Sunil and Shanta from CWIN were still very committed and enthusiastic about the idea and we decided we could go ahead with actors from Aarohan, the children from CWIN and perhaps one or two of the Shuvatara children who wanted desperately to be independently involved.

Then Sunil stopped e-mailing me and despite attempts to contact him through other sources, he was out of touch for over a year, from August 2002 to the end of 2003. During that time, I understand, he was heavily committed to his drama school and working for the ILO, then the company toured to Denmark and Russia. Looking at his website much later, I could begin to appreciate the extent of the company's commitments and how small a part *Rivers of Shame* played in the overall scheme of his work. Despite him telling me that email has created a 'shrinking world', we still have problems connecting, which makes negotiating an international tour overwhelmingly difficult.

Shanta from CWIN continued to write for some time telling me plaintively, 'you are the only one serious about this project.' Anju and other Shuvatara pupils sent occasional wistful messages. Haushala and Galaxy loyally e-mailed me though this has become less frequent after they left school. Galaxy came to England with her family in 2006 and we met several times. Initially homesick for Nepal she is now in Canada training to be a doctor. Both girls stayed true to the spirit of the idea. They were both involved in Save the Children projects on girls' harassment or 'eve teasing'.

Galaxy says the play was the best day of her life. She sent me the report she wrote for the school magazine to include as a footnote in my thesis. It is brimful of emotion. Haushala wanted to train as an actor. They tried for some time to contact Sunil. Only he can restage the play.

I do not know if we will ever pull this off and see the play on an English stage. It's a dream – sometimes dreams are fulfilled, sometimes with the best will in the world they are impossible to fulfil. The dead hand of politics hovers over all this. I hesitate to conjecture too much but I believe we rocked the boat more than was expected. I know there are many things I am not party to that have gone on since my departure and what happens in Nepal over the next few years will determine a great deal more.

Urged to submit a report to the school for the ILO shortly after my return, I felt the necessity of a follow-up evaluation. None seemed likely to materialise from the school so I drafted a questionnaire, e-mailed it to Nepal for comments and waited for its return. I particularly wanted to know if the Shuvatara pupils, generally, felt differently about child labour issues when they had finished the performance than before they started. I also wanted to know if they had kept a link with the CWIN children. Given what the ILO had said about process over product it might have been reasonable to assume they would have wished to measure this themselves.

The responses came back six weeks later. I did not expect miracles, having had no control over the distribution and collection of the survey material, but even so the response rate was hugely disappointing. There were only 16 returned questionnaires, some were incomplete and two had been completed by teachers who had played no part in the project. Returns were received from only five out of ten of the CWIN children but, as a percentage of those taking part, this was infinitely better than the schools – 11 returns were all the feedback I got from 28 performers, 12 researchers, 8 backstage crew, 8 musicians and 200 children involved in the initial sensitisation programme.

A clue to the poor response was the completely irrelevant additional question inserted, without reference to me, by the Vice-Principal:- 'List the seven actors and actresses that you found best in order of their performance'. This was an ensemble piece about an issue of international concern, with the aim of changing hearts and minds, but all the Vice-Principal wanted to know was if the school had any budding actors in their midst.

Unable to establish any statistical generalisations from such a low response rate, I did, nonetheless, manage with the other forms of data collection I had amassed - a detailed personal journal, regular e-mails from the Shuvatara pupils, the CWIN co-ordinator and Sunil – to produce a detailed 38 page report for the ILO, who in return sent me a copy of the Nepalaya film. Sadly, the quality was not good and there was little material from the actual performance.

When I enquired, I found the rushes had meantime been sent to the elusive Ray Conway in Ireland, the man who came to the performance in Nepal and first suggested the tour, and a colleague of the man who had so decisively intervened to ensure that it did not happen .

Worse was to follow. Trying to fill in the gaps that had now appeared in my university research project, I asked the ILO if they could mail me the school's report so I could get their take on the project. I was not expecting what I received. Back came a document which announced it was 'compiled and produced' by Chandreyan P Shrestha, the school's Vice-Principal. What I found I was actually looking at was my own report, cut and pasted rather amateurishly in between long sections lifted from my book, together with confidential material I had expressly not made available to the school and which they had found a way of accessing without my permission, despite my deletion of all material before I left. Any critical comments had been air-brushed out.

Quite apart from issues of confidentiality, invasion of privacy and copyright – which clearly mean little in Nepal – was a complete disinterest in outcomes, and a complete absence of original comment. This could be interpreted either as a reluctance to commit the time to producing an original report when it was easier to plagiarise, or, more depressingly, a lack of interest in any attitudinal changes that had taken place. The only real clue to the school's motivation was contained in one of the rare, semi-literate sentences actually written by the Vice-Principal:-

'As we are a school who has always believed in the all-round development of a child we grabbed this opportunity by supporting the proposal wholeheartedly with the commitment that in no circumstances would it effect the academic performance of the child.'

Coupled with the question about who was the 'best' actor, it is clear that involvement in the project was, for the Vice-Principal, about the personal development of the school's pupils and the prestige the school acquired from being the first school in Nepal to be involved in only the fourth SCREAM project in the world. It had little, if anything, to do with a commitment to the campaign against child labour.

The report horrified me. The budget on the back page was also a cause for concern. I noted the 'author' received 35,000 rupees as 'co-ordinator'– 10,000 more rupees more than I had been offered. Of the box office income there was no mention. The budget for refreshments, props and set (much of it made by me) looked suspiciously high.

What were my feelings about all this? Initially devastated, then very angry, then very sad. I was saved from cynicism only by the handful of children who have stayed loyal to the idea, who are still helping the CWIN children, who continue to send me wonderful messages.

For what we did was something to be very proud of. For all the obstruction and murky politics, I feel immensely privileged to have been involved in such a vitally important project that moved an audience to utter stillness and has changed, perhaps, a handful of children's lives in a quite profound way. In three months that was no mean feat. I'll settle for that.

2004 onwards......

Since writing these final notes I have completed my MA in Applied Theatre with Manchester University, producing as my thesis 'Life into Drama in Nepal'.

On my return to the UK I persuaded my fellow trekkers to support me in bringing Ram Thapa, the trek leader, over to the UK and made contact with the UK group who were already supporting his orphanage in Nepal. The result of our concerted efforts has been the development of a UK charity, *New Futures Nepal,* which has been immensely successful in raising funds, £300,000 in the first six years, thanks to the extraordinary commitment of my fellow trustees and all our wonderful supporters.

Since the charity's inception we have built a new orphanage for the children on the outskirts of Kathmandu and begun another just over the borders in Kalimpong. We have funded medical treatment which has enabled one child to walk properly for the first time in his life, has rescued the sight of another child, and we provide education for many disabled children who would not otherwise get much of a start in life. The majority of them are female. No surprises there then. If this book covers its cost and makes any money I intend the charity will benefit from it. Look up our website or offer us a donation. There is also a DVD available on our work for which I have supplied the voice-over. Contact us at:- **www.newfuturesnepal.com**

My dream of bringing over Aarohan Theatre Company with a revised version of the play still remains unfulfilled. The complexities of funding a project like this are immense. However, nine young people from

Gurukul, the Aarohan Theatre School, (which Sunil was just setting up in 2002) will take part in Contacting the World 2008, a project which brings young people from 12 youth theatres round the world to the UK to perform together under the auspices of Contact Theatre in Manchester. I am pleased I was able to help make this happen.

Life moves on. In 2004 I visited Brazil and trained with the Theatre of the Oppressed in Rio, worked in the Amazon, and in 2006 spent time in India with Janasanskriti, the Indian Theatre of the Oppressed in West Bengal. I also returned to Nepal to attend the Ibsen Festival organised by Aarohan and had a chance to meet up with many of my former pupils and Raju, one of the CWIN lads, who is now a successful actor and artist.

Haushala is still in Nepal and the main link with Raju. Through her I meet a group of the pupils I have worked with, and even four years after our theatre production it was still an experience they felt keenly. When I told them about the Hope Centre and the work of our UK charity, they immediately wanted to help and organised clothing and bedding collections at their college and visited the centre on several occasions with me. They are the young people who will help build a better Nepal.

Rani remains at the centre of a hugely expanded school. The Kakshapatis now also have a boarding school in the mountains where Chandreyan has been installed. Financially the school has made a huge investment in the country, but from what she says, I do not think the expansion has made Rani happy. The Vice-Principal has done well. He bought a new car shortly after the original ILO project and it is rumoured he has been asked to run a further SCREAM project – I am speechless with indignation at the thought.

In November 2008 I take a group of actors to Nepal for the Kathmandu International Theatre Festival organised by Aarohan Theatre with a production of *Eloquent Protest.* Conceived for Armistice Day as an artist's and writer's response to war, *Eloquent Protest* has been an annual event since 2006 in the UK, ably hosted by veteran anti-war campaigner Tony Benn and co-produced by me for Feelgood Theatre Productions.

The Kathmandu version will invite contributions from other visiting companies. Sadly, a common history of war is something we all share.

And then what? Well, I thought I would continue my journey and see more of the world, for I should warn anyone considering following in my footsteps that you may never feel settled again.

My experiences in Nepal have changed me. I am more conscious than ever before of living in the developed world and our gross over-consumption of the world's resources and I cannot defend it in any shape or form or even enjoy it now. My driving force is to continue to make a difference in whatever way I can and encourage others to do the same. It is something we all dream of doing. Nepal handed me that chance. Despite advancing age and the maddening tendency of my body to let me down from time to time, I will still keep following that dream. Life is short. There is much to do.

Hazel Roy, March 2008

Thanks

This book could not have been written without the help of many people. I would like to thank particularly, Rani at Shuvatara for housing me during my time in Nepal, for her friendship, generosity, and the opportunity to become involved in such an important project, and to Puspa and Sheila from the Nepalese Association in the UK for their help in locating schools. I would like to thank Rajan at UCEP for his friendship and for giving me the opportunity to teach at the working children's morning programme; to Madhev for his help and support; to Ram and the children of the Hope Centre for being the inspiration for our UK charity *New Futures Nepal;* to Dr Renu for her passionate commitment and inspirational work with young female victims of trafficking; to Shanta, staff and amazing young actors from CWIN (Child Workers in Nepal) without whom our play would have had no heart and no soul; Kiran at Nepalaya films who recorded the whole project and who continues to be a source of inspiration for his invaluable contribution to the struggle for peace in Nepal; and to the staff at the Kathmandu office of the ILO. Most particularly I want to thank my colleague Sunil Pokharel, Artistic Director of Aarohan Theatre for his invaluable collaboration on the SCREAM project and his continuing friendship and support for theatrical networking between our two countries, and the combined cast of *Rivers of Shame*, some of whom I hope to remain friends with for many years to come and who will always hold a special place in my heart. Lastly I have to offer a HUGE thanks to Jane Allen, who picked this book apart, criticised my self-indulgence, improved my English and grammar immeasurably and urged me to cut the book by half (and was right to do so); to my son Dominic Mandrell, for the layout and design, which I can always rely on to be first class; to Sue Croft for her immaculate editing and to Writersworld for making it possible to finally hold the book in my hand.